HOLLYWOOD
HOOPLA

CREATING STARS
AND
SELLING MOVIES
IN
THE GOLDEN AGE
OF
HOLLYWOOD

W9-DIS-533

HOLLYWOOD

PAN

BILLBOARD BOO

An imprint of Watson-Guptill Publications/New Y

RKO
PANTAGES

25TH
Annual
ACADEMY

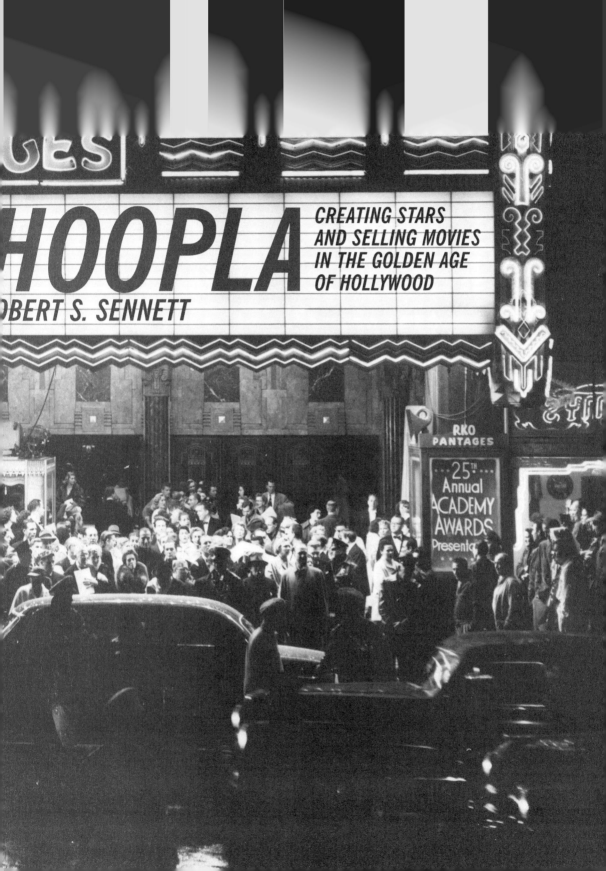

HOOPLA

ROBERT S. SENNETT

*CREATING STARS
AND SELLING MOVIES
IN THE GOLDEN AGE
OF HOLLYWOOD*

RKO
PANTAGES

25TH
Annual
ACADEMY
AWARDS
Presenta

Senior Editor: Bob Nirkind
Editor: Margaret Sobel
Book and cover design: Mirko Ilić Corp.
Production Manager: Ellen Greene

Copyright © 1998 Robert Sennett

First published 1998 by Billboard Books, an imprint of Watson-Guptill Publications,
a division of BPI Communications, Inc., 1515 Broadway, New York, NY 10036

All rights reserved. No part of this publication may be reproduced, stored in a retrieval
system, or transmitted in any form or by any means—electronic, mechanical,
photocopying, recording, or otherwise—without prior permission of the publisher.

Library of Congress Cataloging-in-Publication Data

Sennett, Robert S., 1955–
    Hollywood hoopla : creating stars and selling movies in the golden
    age of Hollywood / Robert S. Sennett.
        p.   cm.
    Includes bibliographical references and index.
    ISBN 0-8230-8331-4
    1. Motion pictures—United States—Marketing. 2. Advertising
    —United States—Motion pictures. I. Title.
    PN1995.9.M29S46   1998
    791.43'068'8-dc21   98-8477
                                                                   CIP

Printed in the USA
First Printing, 1998

1 2 3 4 5 6 7 8 9/04 03 02 01 00 99 98

Page 1
A ring of Paramount starlets, circa 1939—including William Holden, Robert Preston, and Susan Hayward. Photograph courtesy of Photofest, New York.

Pages 2-3
The stars arrive for the 1952 Academy Awards ceremony. Note the lack of traditional bleacher seating for fans and—not coincidentally—a very un-California-like burst of rain. Photograph courtesy of Photofest, New York.

Page 5
Oscar gets buffed. Bronze was scarce during World War II, so the Academy Award statuettes were made of molded plaster and then coated with gold leaf. Photograph courtesy of Photofest, New York.

Page 8
A deserted theater lobby, circa 1920. Most Americans were still one generation or less away from their European roots, and they felt secure—and even pampered—amidst such pseudo-royal splendor. Photograph courtesy of Photofest, New York.

ACKNOWLEDGMENTS

For their help in assembling the illustrations for this book, the author would like to thank the following people: Eileen Kennedy and Elizabeth Ellis at the Department of Prints & Photographs, Museum of the City of New York; Ann Wilkens at the Wisconsin Center for Film & Theater Research, Madison, Wisconsin; and Mary Ann Fitzgerald at the Helene Louise Allen Textile Collection, University of Wisconsin, Madison. I would like especially to thank Howard and Ron Mandelbaum at Photofest in New York, for their ever-helpful expertise and enthusiasm.

In addition, I'd like to offer a special thank you to Bob Nirkind and Margaret Sobel at Billboard Books, and to my agent, Ruth Nathan. And again, to my friend, John Malafronte.

This book is dedicated to the memory of my grandparents, Sol and Hilda Gerber, and Ben and Fay Sinitsky. They sat in the balcony and dreamed, and they worked hard to make their children's dreams—and their children's children's dreams—come true.

CONTENTS

"It would be terrible if somebody did die, but the publicity would be terrific."

—Producer/director William Castle,

after announcing that he was buying insurance in case anyone died from fright from watching his film Macabre *(Castle/Allied Artists, 1958).*

Nirvana to hoopla enthusiasts. The premiere of MGM's Gone with the Wind, at the Loew's Grand, Atlanta, in December 1939 was a perfect reflection of the film itself—expensive, unavoidable, star-laden, and spectacular. *Photograph courtesy of Photofest, New York.*

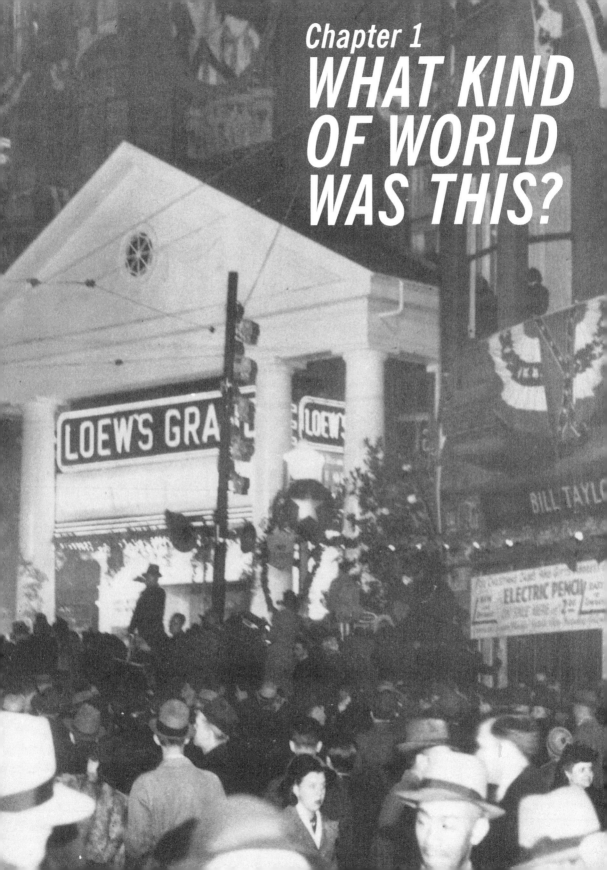

Chapter 1
WHAT KIND OF WORLD WAS THIS?

If you ask anyone today to say the first thing that comes into their mind when you say "Hollywood publicity," you shouldn't have to wait long to hear a response—coming attractions, talk shows, *Entertainment Weekly, Entertainment Tonight.* Our world has become so completely saturated with salesmanship that the selling has literally almost turned invisible. The lines between the thing being sold, the person or organization doing the selling, and the consumer who buys it have worn away. We are what we want.

This world did not exist at the beginning of the twentieth century. Then, the principal method that people used to communicate to one another was speech. Where you went for a good time, how you dressed, the tone of the language (and even the words you used), the kind of soap you bought—all this was primarily communicated from friend to neighbor, from mother to son, one word at a time. There were other methods of communication, of course—books and newspapers were plentiful, and photography was commonplace, if not instantaneous. But not everyone had the time or the ability to read, and a photograph was something you put in the family album or on the mantelpiece. It never moved.

Imagine a world in which there was no such thing as moving images, no advertising "campaigns," no real power over your choice of entertainment, diet, or even career. This is a bit of an exaggeration, of course. Depending upon their financial situation, the town or city they lived in, and the social milieu of their family and community, people all across America had what they felt was a multitude of choices and opportunities. But one hundred years later, surrounded by hundreds of television channels, thousands of products, and millions of CDs, movies, and shows, that world seems impossibly small.

The early publicists, like Edward Bernays and Roger Babson, understood that propaganda, when applied to human desires, was no longer threatening but actually admired. The First World War provided social psychologists with an opportunity to test theories of mass psychology—how to help the government convince Americans, who had recently fled the Continent precisely to avoid fractious conflict, that involvement in the war was not only inevitable but preferable to isolation.

To do this, the U.S. Information Agency (a forerunner of the CIA) commissioned a Committee on Public Information. The Committee quickly concluded that the best and most direct way to influence people's hearts and minds was through imagery—specifically, the movies. There was no sound, only titles—ideal for the millions of illiterate immigrants who were then flooding America's shores. For instilling the basic values of American justice, the need for cooperation, and the civic virtue of fighting for democracy, film was a perfect vehicle. The campaign was a huge success, and the lessons it taught were immediately put into practice by business, commerce, and entertainment.

The key lesson learned was that people are persuaded by symbols sooner than facts, and by visual images sooner than words. In the years following World War I, as public relations firms began sprouting up in New York and across the nation, products began to be sold not in the traditional manner, with testimonials and scientific evidence, but through a new combination of symbols and images—corporate characters such as the Campbell's Kids, or scenes of happy couples with Alcoa products on their table. Chester Berger, a social psychologist who developed the earliest theories of using images to sell products, proclaimed, "Pictures don't illustrate the story…they are the story."

Very quickly, advertising changed from planting and plugging—a salesman's game, dependent upon foot power, pure persistence, and luck—to product placement, celebrity endorsements, and what we now call "lifestyle enhancement"—all no longer dependent upon individuals but upon masses. The goal was not to sell a product but to win public support. It was rightly assumed that once people felt good about a product, they would buy the product in order to feel good about themselves.

The first moviemakers thought of their flickering little images as throwaway novelties—it was the projector they were trying to sell. The idea was that if every home in America bought a Vitascope machine, movies could be sold like razor blades, to be taken home, used up, and discarded. But then the industry began to notice that it was the faces on the screen that people wanted to spend their nickel on, not the box that the face came out of—and Hollywood was born.

If "the business of America is business," as Calvin Coolidge put it in 1922, it was also the business of Hollywood. Motion pictures were a vehicle for making money. If movies entertained millions of Americans and contributed something toward the artistic enlightenment of

*P*aramount starlets shill for *Post* breakfast cereals. These young (and anonymous) women, with
their stylishly curled hair and enthusiastic smiles, were as bland, as wholesome, and as inter-
changeable as the Bran Flakes, Huskies, Grape-Nuts Flakes, and Post Toasties they were holding.
Photograph courtesy of Photofest, New York.

mankind, fine—but profit came first. Any studio or producer who failed to appreciate this fact went broke very quickly.

In its heyday, when the motion picture industry was dominated by the studio production system, Hollywood was emblematic of American business, full of stories of rags-to-riches achievements, the power of individual initiative, and enormous financial remuneration. Yet perhaps the quintessential aspect of Hollywood as a particularly American business was its genius at self-promotion. Indeed, the entire history of Hollywood's "Golden Age" can be viewed as one long advertisement. The product happened to be a movie, carried to glory by a recipe of presold stories; cinematographic effects; printed, spoken, and filmed promotions; fan magazines; publicity gimmicks; and giveaways.

Movies, like other products, can be both good and bad. But good publicity can be applied liberally to anything. A studio on a budget could sing selling words as creative or crass as any silver-plated production. For their entry into 3-D, *It Came from Outer Space* (1953), the art department at Universal designed a garish poster that promised "the most fantastic sights the human eye has ever beheld…xenomorphs from another world." Meanwhile, MGM, which owned not only "more stars than there are in Heaven" but most of the movie screens on earth, could afford to hire July Garland and Mickey Rooney to serve as their opening act for *The Wizard Of Oz* (1939), and send them on tour!

Take, for example, the year 1935. That year, the *Film Daily Yearbook of Motion Pictures* devoted twenty pages to "exploitation" (the commonly used word for non-print advertising), with suggestions running the gamut from special lobby displays and ticket giveaways to beauty contests and sporting event tie-ins. There was no aspect of modern living that the studio publicity departments or theater managers would not try to reach with their advertising campaigns. In 1935, nearly 16,000 movie theaters peppered the American landscape—and all of them got into hoopla in one way or another: holding treasure hunts or baby parades, giving out party favors or candy, or hiring parachutists, midgets, or marching bands.

And this was just front-end publicity, after the picture was finished and ready to go out on the studio's theater circuit. Much more work was needed before the picture was even made. The stars would have to pose for endless portraits, line up interviews with radio and newspaper journalists, and spend nights on the town with their real or imaginary paramours. After the studio art department created the artificial world in which the movie took place, the publicity department would recreate this world in an endless and fanciful series of posters and lobby cards to be sent out alongside the "product," a distillation of a distillation.

Examples abound of the kind of hoopla Hollywood publicists loved to wreak upon the not-so-innocent public. Paramount asked their heads of advertising and exploitation, Bill Thomas and Bill Pine, to come up with a gimmick to sell Mae West's picture *It Ain't No Sin* in 1934. Thomas and Pine went out and purchased fifty African parrots and brainwashed them for weeks with a recording of the film's title. Custom cages were designed for the ill-used birds. As opening night approached, newspaper reporters across America were warned of the approaching migration. Then the Catholic Legion of Decency forced the producers to change the title—Miss West was now starring in *Belle of the Nineties*. No one knows what happened to the birds. Or to Thomas and Pine, for that matter.

There are many other examples. Consider the incredible juggernaut Warner Bros. created for *Dodge City* in 1939. The studio assembled a parade to march down the main street of Dodge City, Kansas, with 40 marching bands and hundreds of horses. Fifty specially decorated airplanes escorted the train of stars as it arrived from Hollywood, while make-believe masked gunmen, alarmingly provided with rounds of blank ammunition, rode down from the surrounding cow towns, firing away. A crowd of over 10,000 people (equal to every man, woman, and child living in Dodge City at the time) witnessed this madcap day of overindulgence. And at Shirley Temple's wedding to John Agar in September 1945, the crowd of over 5,000 grew so unruly that the police had to assume a defensive riot position.

America has a grand tradition of salesmanship. Within the theatrical world, promotion and publicity were already well-established in the vaudeville era when Hollywood was still a peaceful village. But Hollywood hoopla remains the most pervasive, symbolic, and successful hoopla of all. In the Cracker Jack box of American popular culture, Hollywood is everyone's favorite prize. Step right up! ★

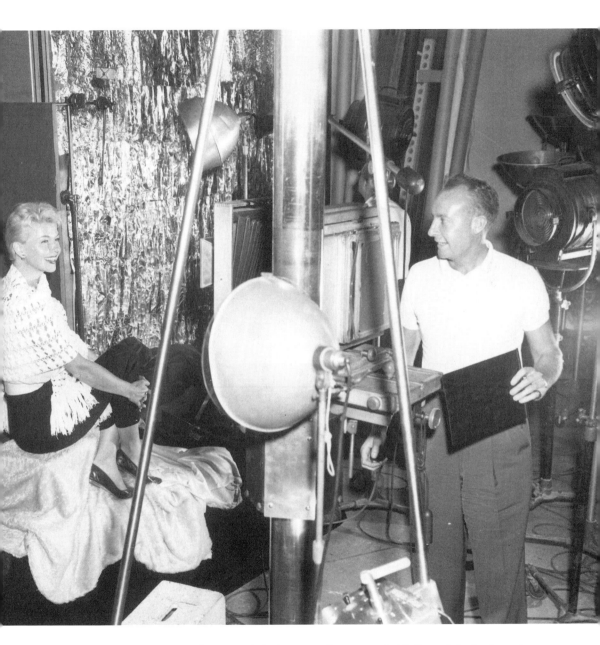

Doris Day's homegrown glamour and plucky personality represented Hollywood stardom's most wholesome incarnation. Here the star cheerfully models a cotton wrap, despite the presence of at least two cameras and three sets of lights. *Photograph courtesy of Photofest, New York.*

Chapter 2
HOORAY FOR HOLLYWOOD!

*T*wo hundred "male animals"—in the form of a Catholic school marching band—serenade moviegoers attending the Milwaukee premieres of *The Male Animal* and *This Was Paris* (both Warner Bros., 1942). *Photograph courtesy of Photofest, New York.*

*T*he American people passed the first half of the twentieth century in a blizzard of self-promotion, advancing the national character and the national spirit to the world. Advertising was the representative business of the age, and motion pictures provided the ideal product. Movies were cheap to make and cheap to sell; they could earn a lot of money, and—best of all—they could be sold to the same consumers over and over again. Not only that, but the audience loved it! What other business could boast of such success?

Hollywood employed every economic, social, and psychological trick it could muster to uncover, develop, maintain, and expand its audience. Frank H. Ricketson, Jr.'s book, *The Management of Motion Picture Theatres,* originally distributed to theater managers at the Fox Inter-Mountain Theatre Management Convention in 1937, became a sort of bible to chain-theater managers across the nation. In its several hundred pages, the book covered everything from booking and equipment leasing to architectural improvements and insurance, but the heart of the work, the middle one hundred pages or so, is dedicated to advertising.

"The theatre manager must be either a natural or a trained psychologist," Ricketson writes, "to be effective in his handling of the fundamentals of attractions and advertising. He must find from study or know instinctively how the public reacts, and he should know why; the better the psychologist, the better the showman. Then why not hire professional psychologists as theatre managers? Because of the danger they might be too pedantic, lean towards complexities, and make laboratories of theatres. Simplicity is an essential of good advertising." The author then continues to offer additional advice to the nascent theater manager regarding newspaper, radio, and outdoor advertising; the theater "front" (marquee, stills, displays, box office); trailers and posters; programs, handbills, and music.

To the eyes of theater managers and studio executives, America was a mythological kingdom with a very limited bank account. For this first generation of moviegoers, there were no statistics to trust and no models to imitate. Competition for the entertainment dollar was going to be tight. This combination of fear and desire lay behind every decision that studio publicity departments had to make. It was imperative for them to maintain the illusion of perfect beauty and absolute control while at the

The Palace Theater, New York, under construction, 1912. Vaudeville was in its fading decades and motion pictures were advancing from novelty to art form when the Palace went up on the corner of Broadway and 47th Street. The Palace Theater was long considered the ultimate venue for any aspiring show biz act. The appeal was so strong that it remained a "mixed house" (alternating live acts with feature films) well into the thirties, when almost every other theater was strictly for movies. Photograph courtesy of The Museum of the City of New York, New York, Wurts Collection.

same time tossing their luck against an immense, unknowable, and fickle public. Again and again, the studios tested their own judgment on the audience, measured the results, and shifted strategies to stay one step ahead of them.

Ezra Goodman reported that it was standard practice for his bosses at *Time* magazine to send copies of his and other interviewers' notes to highly regarded (and anonymous) psychoanalysts in New York and Beverly Hills to obtain evaluations before publication. Presumably the words of "certifiably crazy" stars needed pruning and goosing before they were allowed to be read by the unwashed masses. Creative types were treated like babies. The ill-regarded "talent" (actors, writers, and directors) might schmooze and smile in the LA sun, but the meat of the business, as far as the rulers of the corporations were concerned, was in New York. Only there would one find the money (Wall Street), the manufacturers (for clothes and tie-ins), the publishers (for source material), and the theaters (for anticipating trends) to feed the maw of production.

Metro-Goldwyn-Mayer provides a perfect example of the use of publicity as a vital element of production. The studio's *Who's Who* of 1939 included photographs of stars, featured players, directors, and designers, but there is no one from the publicity department—except on the title page, where the introduction was signed by Howard Strickling and Howard Dietz, heads of the department. The message was clear: "faces" might get the publicity, but publicity makes the faces. Sixteen years later, in the studio's 1956 *Who's Who,* Strickling's self-effacement is complete, as he rattles off numbers he himself was responsible for compiling: "The make-up department is geared to handle as high as 1,200 persons an hour…the wardrobe dept. has handled as many as 5,000 persons in a single day…Electricity, supplied by the company's own electrical plant, could easily light a city of more than 25,000 population…Anything can be manufactured in its shops, from a locomotive to the most microscopically correct device…The casting office has handled as many as 12,000 calls in a day…more than 2 million items of music are contained in the Music Department library."

Hollywood so perfected the twentieth-century art of self-promotion that by the end of the thirties, the business was no longer selling mere product but themselves as well. Cecil B. De Mille was one of the first directors to discover the importance of self-creation, and he managed to parlay his name and his kindly dictatorial image into a template. Thereafter, many other producers and directors modeled themselves after De Mille, turning themselves into brand names—Billy Wilder, Samuel Goldwyn, Michael Todd, Alfred Hitchcock, and Walt Disney. The greatest of these men, certainly in regard to pure publicity and promotion was Disney, who managed to create an entire parallel universe based solely upon his imagination. Amazingly, Disney succeeded in maintaining and eventually expanding this universe long after his own mortal flesh had passed away. The Walt Disney Company, reincarnated in the movies (both live action and animation), on television, and on Broadway, remains the ultimate publicity triumph, the rightful and sometimes even noble heir to MGM.

Even studios with no talent, no theaters, and no money managed to keep afloat in Hollywood's heyday, due to the sheer size of the audience, so huge that no one could sate it. The so-called Poverty Row studios—such as Republic, Monogram, and Tiffany—specialized in audience-pleasing serials, comedies, and westerns. Republic's biggest stars were Roy Rogers and Gene Autry. Between the endless horse operas, the radio shows, and the hit records, the "Singing Cowboys" kept Republic in business straight through the Depression. Studios so poor they had to rent space in Culver City by the day were pleased to find their films filling out double and triple bills all across the nation. Soon the majors jumped into the serial business, sensing a business opportunity, with *The Thin Man* at MGM, *Blondie* at Columbia, and *Charlie Chan* at Twentieth Century-Fox.

Over the years, the studios grew increasingly sophisticated and shrewd in the methods of self-promotion. Tried-and-true techniques (interviews and articles), dependent as they were upon the written word, gave way to more visual and consequently more visceral media, such as puzzles, tie-ins, color posters, and trailers. And—whether blatant or subtle, spoken or signed, free or costly—the key to the studio's overall publicity management was programming.

Nowadays, as pictures are released independently and singly, the concept of programming is incomprehensible, except on the very rare occasions of tributes or festivals. But in the Golden Age, programming

*C*over illustration for the sheet music for "Revenge," from the movie of the same name (United Artists, 1921). Vaudeville was dead, but its influence was still strong—note the ukulele arrangement and the Art Nouveau drawing. *Photograph courtesy of the Wisconsin Center for Film and Theater Research, Madison, Wisconsin.*

was perhaps the most fundamental publicity device that studios had at their command. Basically, a studio program told the audience how to react to a picture before the stars or even the story was known. A huge majority of theaters were owned by one of the studios, and these theaters had to buy the complete program or try to swim on their own, which almost certainly would have led to bankruptcy.

The audience knew how to react to a program and what to expect because they had been indoctrinated to expect a certain hierarchy of pictures. First in importance came the superspecials, "A" pictures with stars and music, booked on the biggest screens for up to two weeks. Below this, there were specials, which included "weepies" or women's pictures like *Johnny Belinda* (Warner Bros., 1948) and historical dramas. A third type of "A" picture, simply called a programmer, was the cheapest kind of action or adventure yarn. Then there were "B" pictures—shorts, serials, and "ethnic" comedies. A typical touring bill, or program, would be booked into several big cities, and would include one superspecial or special and two programmers, plus shorts, serials, newsreels, and cartoons. Everyone, from the studio executive to teenagers on a date, expected the superspecial to be the hit, and the programmers to be at least not boring—and, invariably, this was so. A superspecial that failed to find an audience would be quickly withdrawn and replaced.

A sample program note from the twenties is indicative of what theatergoers expected for their dime. Over the course of a few hours at the Capitol Theatre in New York, the audience could see a travelogue on Venice, a newsreel, a full-length feature, and a Mack Sennett comedy, all sandwiched around three orchestral interludes, two vocalists, and the Capitol Ballet Corps. At smaller venues, like the Coliseum Theatre in Seattle or the Century in Baltimore, the bill would be lighter (and less expensive) but generally followed the same pattern. In the last years of vaudeville, it was perfectly common to find organ soloists, opera singers, harp duos, lecturers, interpretive dancers, acrobats, and barbershop quartets filling in between pictures.

This complete vertical integration from the studios to the theaters (at least until the Supreme Court broke it up after World War II) allowed the publicity departments to carefully plan their promotional campaigns knowing which films would be opening in which cities and theaters months in advance. They did this not only for the big releases, as is the present case, but for specials, programmers, and shorts. This predictability was somehow liberating. When everyone from mogul to matron knew exactly what he or she was going to see from week to week, they looked forward to it with keen anticipation.

The studios rightly concluded that anyone paying her way into a superspecial was a captive audience. They loaded up the bill with enough filler to keep the seats warm for hours. When a lame remake of *Of Human Bondage* went out in 1946, Warner Bros. included a sports short *(The Riding Hannefords),* clips from their own musicals *(Musical Memories),* two cartoons *(Johnny Smith & Poker Huntas* and *Acrobatty Bunny,* featuring Bugs Bunny), a travelogue *(Down Singapore Way),* and a parade of bathing beauties *(Beach Days).* Similarly, the bill for *The Oklahoma Kid* (1939) included a historical short on Abraham Lincoln, a musical review, a big band number, a nature short, and two cartoons.

Costumes were cheap and easy to reproduce, so the studios had no qualms offering pieces of them to *Picture Show* magazine as giveaway prizes for their readers. Anyone clever enough to solve a simple acrostic or spell "Merle Oberon" could win Frank Sinatra's sailor hat from *On the Town* (MGM, 1949), Victor Mature's headband from *Samson and Delilah* (Paramount, 1951), Erich von Stroheim's gloves from *Sunset Boulevard* (Paramount, 1950), or Leslie Caron's ballet slippers from *An American in Paris* (MGM, 1951). Pet owners were ripe for exploitation as well, since moviegoers could be counted on to buy something for their beloved animal that they couldn't afford for themselves. For *The Return of Rin-Tin-Tin* (Eagle-Lion, 1947), fans were offered a tie-in with Gaines dog food, packages of animal crackers, and special discounts at a local K9 Corps–affiliated veterinarian.

Not even God was immune from being asked to do a little promo work when it was needed. When Warner Bros. released their inspirational *One Foot in Heaven* (1941), they invited the editor-in-chief of the Protestant *Christian Herald,* Daniel A. Poling, to preview the picture. The result was a ringing endorsement. At first, Poling admitted to his parishioners that he was inclined to refuse the invitation or ignore it. But this, he felt, would be dishonest, a condemnation without basis. In the end, Warner Bros. had nothing to fear. Mr. Poling gave glowing reviews:

Still from the trailer for Notorious (RKO, 1946). A pure example of the signature Hollywood advertising style of (big, bigger, biggest!), with the customary disregard for proper grammar or punctuation. Photography courtesy of Photofest, New York.

"vital, simple, rich with humor, and appealing to all ages and faiths."

Showing a bit of a competitive edge, Poling also admitted that part of his reason for supporting Warner Bros. in their endeavor came directly as a result of the success of Warner Bros.' *Knute Rockne–All American* (1940) and *Boys' Town* (MGM, 1938) amongst Catholic moviegoers. He even applauded the studio's decision to hire Dr. Norman Vincent Peale as technical advisor, and concluded with an improvised prayer: "May the box office returns justify those who have, at their own risk, invested more than a million dollars in this unique production. May this verdict be so conclusive that *One Foot in Heaven* will become the first of a cycle and help usher in a new day of better pictures for America." Can't you just hear Jack Warner muttering, "Amen?" As if this was still not enough, the studios also advised their exhibitors to contact local religious organizations to offer free previews to the clergy in the hope of garnering additional endorsements during the Sunday sermons. Warner Bros.' press book for the film included a church model-building contest, presumably for the benefit of the young sacred architects in their audience.

Programming allowed the studios to carefully time the release of their tie-in merchandising to maximize exposure. The two most important areas for tie-ins—not only because of the financial rewards but also because of their effect on the popular culture—were fashion and music. Songs that were to be featured in upcoming major releases needed to be recorded and released to radio stations several weeks before opening night. MGM radio head Les Peterson would meet once each week with the studio's musical director, Johnny Green, to go over the latest songs and pick the ones they thought could become hits. Meanwhile, the studio costume designers would meet with the buyers from the most prestigious and influential clothing manufacturers to introduce dress patterns, accessories, and color schemes months ahead of the release date.

Nowhere is the power and the transparency of Hollywood publicity more apparent than in the Academy Awards. The "Oscars" began as a publicity ploy, and they have never seriously strayed too far from that goal. When the first awards dinner was held in the Biltmore Hotel in Los Angeles in May 1928, the industry was at the nadir of one of its periodic artistic and financial crises. Labor disputes had broken out on the sets; sound was threatening the status quo, and an air of impending fiscal doom had settled over the town. The Academy of Motion Picture Arts and Sciences was formed by the producers at the studios as a rival professional organization whose intent was to deliberately undercut the burgeoning union movement. At the same time, it was hoped that by giving out glitzy, competitive prizes, they could distract the public from the fluctuating quality of the pictures.

Over the years, the specific intent of the Academy Awards has more or less become a generalized valentine to the business. The television show has become associated with fancy dresses and long-winded speeches—a night of self-congratulation devoid of the usual petty battles. The awards have never been taken too seriously—and then only as financial bargaining chips, not as prizes—and their impact as a publicity tool is now limited to the few films which enter into competition and does not apply to the industry as a whole. For the simple truth of the matter is that there no longer exists "the industry as a whole"—it is international, independent, and fragmented, and under such circumstances, real unity cannot exist.

But in the Golden Age, the industry did speak with one voice. True, this was largely because contrary voices were muffled—but one voice is much easier to sell than one hundred. How else could we understand that not only God, but even the Second World War, was considered good for business? Indeed, in 1943 *Variety* reported:

> Morale means entertainment; entertainment means making a heavy heart lighter—a strained day of work or warfare just a shade brighter. The man at the front is sustained by a song on his lips; the men and women on the home front, ceaselessly twisting bolts and riveting steel, are bolstered by a laugh. To dwell on "morale" may be something akin to coining a cliche, but whatever its label, it's entertainment—and entertainment is Show Business.

Hollywood was in its glory days during the War, and the publicity mills did their best to show it. No star would object to having his or her picture taken "with the boys," and when the time came to distribute the

Marilyn Monroe and Jane Russell etch their way into the Walk of Fame in front of Grauman's Chinese Theater, circa 1953. Photograph courtesy of Photofest, New York.

latest picture at home or overseas, such generosity and goodwill was not forgotten. Warner Bros. especially took it upon themselves to place their product in the midst of the patriotic fervor, turning out *This Is the Army, Mission to Moscow, Watch on the Rhine, Destination Tokyo* (all 1943), *Hollywood Canteen* (1944), *To Have and Have Not* (1945), and, of course, *Casablanca* (1942), all heavily promoted in *American Legion* and *Foreign Service* magazines. But Warner Bros. was not alone—every studio took a crack at the enemy. Alfred Hitchcock succeeded in the improbable task of turning Claude Rains into a Nazi in *Notorious* (RKO, 1946), although by then the War was over.

We now see, through the looking glass of several decades, that both war and Hollywood thrive on illusion. But illusion is not always a dirty word. It is wrong to deceive people about one's actual intent in order to exploit them—as did occur both in the Vietnam War and in the financial scandals which plagued the motion picture industry with some regularity since the fifties. But illusions can also be inspiring. They can spark the imagination, ennoble the soul, and empower people to accomplish their dreams. The greatest illusion created by the Second World War was that it was a "good" war, a justifiable defense of freedom against tyranny. And it seems as if the fundamental elements of this illusion were true.

In the same way, Hollywood in the forties was also a grand illusion, a "good" illusion. War is real, and movies are not—but in the Golden Age of Hollywood, from the birth of sound in 1929 to the end of the studio-owned theater chains in 1948, movies provided American culture with potent illusions, and used these illusions to create powerful, honorable, generous (but also flawed, destructive, and treacherous) characters. If you wish to influence a lot of people, you need to create common illusions. In war, this is called propaganda; in Hollywood, it is called publicity.

Publicity never looks better than when it is noble, and the War offered Hollywood the opportunity to out-noble the best of them. It was a moment of acute equilibrium, poised between the champagne-filled bathtubs of an earlier age and the fractured, incoherent world yet to come. It was a moment when unity was needed—unity and balance and a belief in the rightness of the world, however illusory. ★

Rita Hayworth poses for a publicity still for You'll Never Get Rich (Columbia, 1941). Hayworth was extraordinarily photogenic—perhaps the most photogenic film star ever—and this carefully posed shot is artful and alluring. Note that the Movie Story, Movie Stars, and Stardom magazine props still have the studio advertising department labels on them, and that some secretary has circled the title of the movie being advertised to aid in filing. *Photograph courtesy of Photofest, New York.*

Chapter 3
A CAST OF THOUSANDS: HOW STARS WERE BORN

MOVIE STORY MAGAZINE

NOVEMBER

FRED ASTAIRE
RITA HAYWORTH
"YOU'LL NEVER GET RICH"

The Hollywood studios developed the star system when they discovered, to their great glee and profit, that movie stars could be marketed as successfully as soap. Early filmmakers had depended upon a steady supply of stage actors. For the most part, these actors were ill-suited to film style, which required small gestures, virtual immobility, and a talent to communicate emotions through the eyes. The new style—Hollywood style—needed icons. Thus, ordinary human beings became transfigured. They became movie stars.

Stardom was completely calculated. An ingenue with an interesting face would initially be typed as "the other woman," "the girl next door," "the dutiful wife," or "the zany debutante." Scripts would be developed, screen tests made, exhibitors polled, publicity photographs made. If the studio was relatively poor and the starlets had no discernible talent, the result would be a Rochelle Hudson or a Judith Barrett—two young women who received all the advantages but could not capitalize on them. But when the studio machinery clicked and the "dame was game," the sky was the limit. The female stars were most often the victims of these efforts, but men were not immune to this treatment, so long as—per the social rules of the day—they were not portrayed as weak or manipulated.

Each of the major motion picture studios in Hollywood utilized similar star-making machinery. After the talent was identified and named, an imaginary biography was invented—one that would add luster to the "type" of star that was desired. The star would then be assigned a studio publicist, who would be responsible for distributing the fake bio to all the newspapers, magazines, and columnists, as well as escorting the new charge around town to parties, premieres, and nightclubs. Next would come a shopping spree to assemble an appropriate wardrobe and a session with one of the studio portrait photographers.

Once the star was identified, presented, and placed in the proper niche, it was time to put him or her to work. Stories were developed for the star, not the other way around, for it was imperative that the star never be required to act out of character or against type. Constant polling of the picture magazines, exhibitors, and newspapers produced a strict ranking system which controlled every element of an actor's involvement in a picture. The size of your part depended upon whether you were a

*M*ickey Rooney and Bette Davis being crowned King and Queen of Hollywood in 1940 by columnist Ed Sullivan. Phony awards helped boost a star's box office appeal, and the victims were often just as willing as the perpetrators to engage in this brand of boosterism. Davis grew tired of it within a few years; Rooney never did. Photograph courtesy of Photofest, New York.

supporting player (who had a contract that ran from week to week), a stock player (who got six months), or a featured actor (whose contract could last for a year). An actor could work for a decade, rising up from supporting roles to featured parts, before receiving star billing.

The history of Hollywood is littered with stories of stars—in fact, a case could be made that the real history of Hollywood is nothing but star stories. Of course, many truly magnificent films were made without stars, where the story was gripping and the emotions were satisfying and true. But where the film medium is unique, where it resembles no other art form, is in the power of the close-up and the icon of the star. Throughout the Golden Age of Hollywood, making stars, becoming a star, and connecting with the stars was a national obsession and the mantra of the industry. Stars were built, bought, and sold—and studio publicity departments were deeply involved in the process every step of the way.

Stars could be "imported" and transformed, as the nation imported and transformed the immigrants of previous generations. Prominent radio performers were invited to California, where writers would be hired to "visualize" their acts. Vaudeville personalities would be placed under contract and then handed scripts that stripped their routines until nothing original remained. Great stars of the Yiddish theater, such as Eddie Cantor and Fanny Brice, and their honorary heirs, The Marx Brothers, were anglicized and reduced to doing slapstick, chases, and novelties, leaving little of the fully realized performances they had created for the stage. The Marx Brothers survived and even flourished because they had the luck of working with good writers. A radio star like Bing Crosby could make the switch because he knew how to act.

The road to stardom was always crowded with traffic. The Western Association of Motion Picture Advertisers (WAMPAS) held a contest every year for a young actress who showed promise. The WAMPAS "Baby Stars," as they were named, included Clara Bow (1924), Mary Astor (1926), Joan Blondell (1931), and Ginger Rogers (1932). The fan magazines were filled with earnest advice for young girls (and, presumably, boys). "Go to a recording studio or your local record shop and make a record of your voice...do a scene from a play and send your record or tape-recording to me at Metro-Goldwyn-Mayer," wrote producer Mervyn

LeRoy. Studio publicity departments set up satellite post offices to receive, screen, and respond to fan letters, which arrived daily by the tens of thousands. The stars themselves (most likely with the assistance of their own public relations staff) never hesitated to release the most pathetic or worshipful letters to the press and make certain that the powers-that-be were aware of their numbers. Universal actually asked their starlets to sign a "cheesecake" clause in their contracts, requiring suitably endowed female newcomers to "display said charms in publicity pictures as well as on the screen for the first five years of the duration of her contract."

The star treatment was ruthless, impersonal, and universal—no actor in Hollywood could gain any measure of success without submitting to the demands of the publicity department. A few, like Katharine Hepburn and Spencer Tracy, managed at least a truce, while others, like Clark Gable and Bette Davis, fought every step of the way (to even greater publicity). The vast majority of movie stars played the game as best they could, and a few, the very cream of Hollywood royalty, actually enjoyed it and built their entire careers out of a public relations house of cards.

Joan Crawford is at the top of this list. From her flapper beginnings in *Our Dancing Daughters* (MGM, 1928) to her status as camp icon in *Whatever Happened to Baby Jane?* (Warner Bros., 1962), no star ever loved the glare of stardom—or manipulated it to better effect—than Crawford. She never stepped out of character, ever. Louella Parsons noted that Crawford was "the only star I know who manufactured herself. She drew up a blueprint and outlined a beautiful package." Miss Crawford made a conscious attempt to influence fashion and social behavior. She would arrange her own personal appearances, which would have to be scheduled to the minute. She called the press continually to offer her opinions on everything from her latest film to the State of the Union. And she got people to listen. If Joan Crawford endorsed your perfume, your luggage, or even your soda pop (she eventually married the owner of Pepsi-Cola), you were golden.

Rita Hayworth was another brilliantly manufactured star, although in her case her stardom was less her own doing than that of her Svengali. Every firsthand account of Hayworth's beginnings as a Mexican dancer,

Barbara Stanwyck makes a personal appearance in support of Clash by Night *(RKO, 1952)*. At the time, most stars, no matter how big, considered it part of their responsibility to the studio and to their fans to visit theaters showing their films to raise money for charity, sign autographs, support local businesses, and—not incidentally—to show off their sense of fashion and their charm.

Photograph courtesy of Photofest, New York.

born Margarita Cansino, points out that she was pathologically shy and unversed as an actress, and that it took the manipulations of several men—all of whom were married to her at one time or another—to effect the transformation. First there was Eddie Judson, who changed her hair from black to red and changed her name from Margarita to Rita, then tried to blackmail her when she tried to leave him. Next there was Orson Welles, who changed her hair again (from red to blonde, but her fans didn't like it and she changed it back to red) and tried to turn Rita into a mysterious siren. Finally there was Aly Khan, the billionaire prince, who swept Hayworth into an international crowd that terrified her. At their wedding in Monte Carlo in 1949, the world got an early glimpse of the temerity of the paparazzi, who hunted the couple like wild game.

Miss Hayworth was never great shakes as an actress, but no other star ever photographed so brilliantly or moved across the screen with such guileless assurance. As so often occurs with the most unique of film stars, Margarita Cansino *became* Rita Hayworth—the shy Mexican girl completely disappeared when the cameras were turned on. Just seeing her sing "Put the Blame on Mame" in *Gilda* (Columbia, 1946) is proof enough of her abilities as a singer and a dancer. When the U.S. Army tested a hydrogen bomb over the Bikini Islands in 1947, the crew named their missile "Gilda" and taped a pinup of Hayworth to its side. Again, Parsons: "To Miss Hayworth's studio, it amounted to the most literally earth-shattering free plug in the history of the world."

Some stars burned brightly despite a definite lack of maturity and common sense. Magazine reporter and Hollywood columnist Ezra Goodman chronicled Kim Novak's fitful climb to the top in his book, *The Fifty-Year Decline and Fall of Hollywood.* According to Goodman, Novak knew she could not act, but Columbia placed an inordinate amount of pressure upon her to be a star. One studio associate said to Goodman:

> The whole thing is a horrible strain on Kim. She knows she isn't an actress, but she's ambitious. She cracks up under pressure. She throws up, gets carsick and airsick. She throws tantrums and hysterical fits. She is now driving everyone at the studio nuts. She will go nuts herself in the next five years, or at least wind up on a psychiatric couch.

Novak's lack of confidence did not prevent her from making threats to her boss, Harry Cohn, head of Columbia Pictures, or from continuing her tantrums on the set when things did not always go exactly her way. Novak was assigned a personal photographer, a drama coach, a nutritional advisor, and a gym instructor, to little avail. Ezra Goodman reported: "While Novak and a studio publicity girl were being driven across the Alps, the chauffeur said to Miss Novak, 'Miss Kim, I have had the honor and the privilege to drive some of the greatest dignitaries of our time—the Duke and Duchess of Windsor, Field Marshal Montgomery, and also your President.' Novak replied, in all seriousness, 'You mean Harry Cohn?'"

Lana Turner was another star created out of whole cloth. Miss Turner was apparently a corn-fed innocent. Moguls like Mervyn LeRoy like to describe young Judy Turner as "scared to death... nothing like she is today. She had no poise, no assurance. Her hair was dark. It wasn't combed and I used to tell her it looked like a mattress." Louella Parsons reported the results of Lana Turner's marriage to bandleader Artie Shaw and of Shaw's subsequent attempts to raise the starlet's intellectual bar a bit. Turner told Parsons, "I know that I ought to be interested in these things. After all, I didn't have too much education. But you know something, Louella, all they did was make me sleepy." To which Parsons replied, "It was hard to adjust to reading Kant instead of the menu at Romanoff's."

Marilyn Monroe had the same problem finding her niche. She bleached her hair blonde and posed nude for magazines, which caught the attention of Howard Hughes. Hughes ordered a test at the studio he owned, RKO, but producer Darryl Zanuck was so unimpressed with the star-to-be that he canceled the appointment, and Monroe had to be snuck into the studio lot to have her test made. She was eventually signed and then dumped by Zanuck, signed and dumped by MGM, and then signed and dumped and re-signed by Twentieth Century-Fox. It took personal intervention on the part of Fox studio head Spyros Skouras, in the form of taking Monroe as a dinner escort to an exhibitors' meeting, before she got a break. The studio still couldn't figure out how to use her in a picture, but in the meantime the folks in publicity arranged for a string of racy promo shots to blanket every news syndicate and magazine in the country. Miss Monroe was a star before her name had ever appeared above a title.

Other female stars of greater talent and circumspection than Marilyn Monroe or Lana Turner entered into the Hollywood publicity fray more carefully. Grace Kelly was notoriously bad copy—she wouldn't do "leg shots" and constantly lectured her interviewers on religious and moral matters. Her mother wrote the only official account of her engagement to Prince Rainier of Monaco. Dinah Shore was by all reports a perfectly happy, professionally content, and definitely second-level movie star, although she once found herself the victim of a completely fabricated suicide-attempt story. At first, Greta Garbo managed to avoid the usual indignities by refusing to allow any studio portraits that were not character studies from her costume dramas. When this became too much for her, she retired altogether and never subjected herself to a jot of public relations again.

A few stars found that they had the admirable ability to manipulate the press as well as the press manipulated others. Lorraine Day couldn't get a good part from her studio until she trumpeted her Mexican divorce from her husband, Leo Durocher. Her willfulness cast her right into type, and the newly single Miss Day had a prosperous few years playing independent-minded women. Carole Lombard vividly demonstrated her skill at controlling her audience to William Holden. In later years, Holden told Ezra Goodman, "Miss Lombard went shopping down Fifth Avenue with a studio publicist. The publicist said to her: 'It's amazing. No one recognizes you.' 'That's simple,' she replied, 'It's because I don't want them to.' Then she tossed back her blonde hair and swung her mink coat and people started asking her for autographs. 'See what I mean?' she said, and then she quietly went back to window shopping." Mae West was a walking catalogue of provocative behavior, and the fact that she was taken seriously only increased her desire to see how much she could get away with.

Stars had fan clubs, usually instigated by the studio and easily manipulated for the studio's own benefit. At one point, Deanna Durbin's club had fifty branches. Clark Gable's club wanted a button from his tuxedo; Fred Astaire's wanted the wishbone from his Christmas turkey. When over one hundred and fifty members of the Jane Withers Fan Club arrived at Fox's gate and found it locked, alert folks at Warner Bros. across the street spotted them and invited them in. The Jane Withers Fan Club promptly offered to change allegiance to a Warner Bros. ingenue of the studio's choice.

Of course, star stories can only be told in retrospect. The number of actors who failed in their attempt to become stars is legion, and their stories never get published. Sociologist Hortense Powdermaker provides a glimpse of this life in her account of "Miss Frustrated," an anonymous aspiring starlet. In Powdermaker's 1950 account, "Miss Frustrated" has been trying to break into the business for seven years, without any sign of success. This actress has no professional experience to speak of, yet she speaks glowingly of herself and her skills and is convinced that her lucky break is just around the corner. At the time of her interview, "Miss Frustrated" is working part-time to make ends meet, and using whatever extra money she can scrape up to put small advertisements for herself in the trade papers. Powdermaker is impressed by this obviously deluded ingenue's sense of determination and self-willed happiness, but ominously concludes: "There are many others like Miss Frustrated."

Men in Hollywood fared little better than women when it came to being exploited by the studios, but because they were men they were allowed greater freedom according to the moral double standard of the day. Thus Errol Flynn could remain one of Warner Bros.' top stars despite tales of constant debauchery. According to Flynn, the studio tried assigning one of its top publicists, Blake McElroy, to guard Flynn on a trip to Manhattan, but the actor shook McElroy off within twenty-four hours and ended up in bed with a Russian princess. While on tour promoting *Captain Blood* (Warner Bros., 1935), Flynn faked a medical emergency and disappeared for three days, only to turn up a few floors above the studio's own rented suite, drunk and accompanied by hired "escorts." It has never been determined how many of these stories about Errol Flynn were actually true, and how many were elaborations or fabrications provided by Flynn himself.

Some male stars were most accommodating. Paramount asked Bing Crosby to pin his ears back to make him appear more handsome. In exchange for frequent plugging, Gig Young allowed his press agent and all his agent's friends to sign Young's name to their lunch bills. Richard

A page from the Jezebel press book. Product endorsements were part of a star's contractual duties in the Golden Age of Hollywood publicity. For Jezebel (Warner Bros., 1938), star George Brent chimed in for Calox Tooth Powder. His two quotes, plus endorsements from "many Hollywood dentists" were offered in the press books for submission to newspapers and magazines across the nation in conjunction with the release of the movie. *Photograph courtesy of the Wisconsin Center for Film and Theater Research, Madison, Wisconsin.*

Widmark, in his characteristically straightforward manner, said, "Movies advertise to sell their product, and I am their product, along with the picture... It's a selling job, like selling anything—a refrigerator, a book, or nail polish." A previously unknown actor named Bill Boyd made forty-four films between 1935 and 1944 as Hopalong Cassidy, and got rich by actively participating in his own merchandising. There were Hopalong cartoons, comic books, guns, and hats. Boyd made personal appearances; started his own club newspaper, *The Trooper;* spun out to the new medium of television; and ended up with over seventy million dollars. Actors so inclined could make a few extra bucks endorsing everything from shaving cream to automobiles.

The most characteristic male impulse in the Hollywood star game was the snub or insult. Frank Sinatra fervently believed there was no publicity like bad publicity, and seemed to prove his point by walking out on his wives or slugging reporters with alarming regularity. The "Rat Pack" was started by Humphrey Bogart and eventually included not only Sinatra but restaurateur Mike Romanoff, David Niven, songwriter Jimmy Van Heusen, Peter Lawford, Sammy Davis Jr., singer Joey Bishop, and Dean Martin, as well as honorary female members such as Lauren Bacall, Judy Garland, and later, Garland's daughter, Liza Minnelli. They all loved to razz anyone who would listen, and their act—as boorish, rich social drinkers who liked to live hard and with a certain amount of black honor—became a publicity myth all its own.

Erich von Stroheim was an extremely intelligent and very cultivated man, but he loved to play the role of the Mad Hun. Ezra Goodman arranged an interview with von Stroheim for a young girl freshly hired by United Press International. The girl, doing her job, had been asking questions, and von Stroheim was growing increasingly irritated. He had also been drinking. "Finally," Goodman reports, "the girl asked, 'What is your hobby, Mr. von Stroheim?' The great director, who had by then knocked off a dozen or more shots of Scotch neat, looked at her menacingly and replied in one brief, pungent, Anglo-Saxon verb. The young lady was so taken aback that she ran out of the apartment, leaving her notebook and purse behind her, and von Stroheim was out one wire service interview."

As with everything else, Goodman was a very astute critic of the glory and the idiocy of star-making machinery. He delights in revealing that Shirley Temple's divorce was reported "exclusively" first by Louella Parsons, then Florabel Muir, and then Edith Gwynne, and he notes, "No wonder Shirley and her spouse went phfft—she must have been speaking all the time on the telephone." Goodman's book chronicles the Debbie Reynolds–Eddie Fisher–Elizabeth Taylor story as it filtered its way through the trades. At first, *Motion Picture* tried to portray Reynolds as a victim in "The Terrible Fear of a Divorced Woman." When this tack failed to spur readership, they switched back to sex, running an article called "Debbie's Secret Suitor," which intimated an illicit romance, despite the fact that Miss Reynolds was already engaged to Harry Karl at the time.

Goodman continues in this direction for another three pages, quoting *Modern Screen, Movieland,* and *TV Time* as each of them chime in about Miss Reynolds' predicament. But for every honest cynic like Ezra Goodman, there were a hundred innocents for whom stardom was the highest accolade to which a human being could aspire. Adela Rogers St. Johns, whose prose could be as grandiose as her name, writes her account of Gloria Swanson's arrival at the premiere of *Madame Sans Gene* (Paramount, 1925) as if she has just witnessed Napoleon's coronation. She describes crowds jamming the streets for ten blocks in either direction, cheers rising like the roar of a football crowd, and then the Great Lady herself, draped in silver lamé and diamonds and escorted by her new, blue-blooded husband, the Marquis de la Falaise de la Coudrey.

Without a trace of irony, Miss St. Johns writes: "I saw men standing on their seats, waving their arms, other women tearing off their orchids and flinging them into the aisle for Gloria Swanson to walk on—and I saw Mack Sennett frankly wiping the tears from his proud face. One of his girls had certainly made good."

The life of a Hollywood movie star was Byronic, not ironic. ★

Chapter 4
THE LITTLE PEOPLE: GOSSIP COLUMNS AND FAN MAGAZINES

L ouella Parsons (right) poses with radio and film star Gracie Allen (Mrs. George Burns) at the Brown Derby restaurant in Hollywood. The hats and jewels suggest they were not captured having a light lunch by chance, but had meticulously planned the session with the photographer well in advance. Photograph courtesy of Photofest, New York.

*F*or an industry so completed defined by images, Hollywood was always strangely dependent upon words. First, of course, there were the words heard coming from the screen—the scripts. Someone had to give the actors something to say. Scriptwriters, however, rarely had enough clout to influence a star's career or help make money for the studio. But the words that were written about Hollywood represented an entirely different situation. During the heyday of the Hollywood studios, the gangs of newspaper columnists, radio reporters, and magazine writers who worked the silver screen circuit were almost always among the most powerful people in town.

In 1939, there were over three hundred members of the press on the Hollywood beat. This included nationally syndicated columnists such as Hedda Hopper and Louella Parsons, East Coast newspaper reporters like Walter Winchell and Dorothy Kilgallen, influential local reporters such as Edith Gwynne of the *Hollywood Reporter* and Mike Connolly of *Variety,* as well as copy editors looking for pictures and items to run in the fan magazines *(Modern Screen, Photoplay).* In addition, there were "women's magazines" that featured profiles and interviews of Hollywood stars *(Redbook, McCall's)* and general-interest magazines that put stars on the covers to boost circulation *(Look, Life).*

This was only the first tier, the A-list. The people who worked at these places received exclusive interviews, passes to private screenings, and invitations to all the best parties. Beyond them lay the dailies in the hinterlands and the foreign press corps, which would have to fight for the crumbs. Not that the crumbs were insubstantial—in the days when ink and radio were the only means of communicating to the public, movie stars continually crisscrossed the world making personal appearances to promote their work. All across America and the world, newsprint needed to be filled with reports of stars working tirelessly for their favorite charity, selling bonds, or cutting the ribbon for some new bridge, building, or monument.

It all began with Sime Silverman. Silverman was barely thirty years old when he decided that America's booming entertainment business could use a newspaper to call its own. The year was 1905, and the paper was *Variety. Variety* offered the fledgling movie industry a sort of legitimacy. Favoring unstuffy writing and with a proclivity to puff up every

Walter Winchell tells it like it is. Winchell's East Coast success as a reporter was never really duplicated out West, and eventually his mean-spiritedness and political paranoia turned him into an outcast. Photography courtesy of Photofest, New York.

aspect of the world of show business, *Variety* became the model for what constituted reporting in Hollywood for decades to come. Silverman and his staff dreamed up *Variety's* inimitable headline style ("Bette Boffo in Warner's Weeper"). By the usual route of perverse logic, *Variety's* lighthearted tone caused everyone in show business to take it very, very seriously. As Hollywood boomed, the stakes grew higher, and the writers and editors of *Variety* loved to raise the bar. Silverman died in 1933, but his spirit lives on in the language ("d.j.," "legit," "hit," "flop," and "baloney" are all *Variety*-inspired words) and in the brand of breezy, confident hucksterism which still inhabits the best of show business.

Throughout the twenties, the studios depended heavily upon the fan magazines for star-related publicity. The first and most successful of these was *Photoplay,* edited by James R. Quirk. *Photoplay* ran long articles and profiles on the studio's top personalities and produced hardcover annuals full of glossy full-page photographic portraits. Imitations quickly proliferated: *Modern Screen, Screen Stars, Movieland, Screenland,* ad nauseam. All of them would mine the same territory— ghostwritten "features" about the lives of the stars (largely fictionalized) enlivened with romance, advertisements, and fan club offers. Each tried to distinguish itself from its competitors in some way or another. *Motion Picture,* for example, sold four-by-five-inch photographs of stars for ten cents apiece. Bigger and better shots, mounts, and frames were available for more money, of course.

The fan magazines were extremely popular and resolutely lowbrow. This combination caused them to be particularly disliked by Hollywood's own. The average fan magazine writer was described by one anonymous press agent as "eight thousand years old. She had a bladder condition. She would come to the studio and bring her stinking, lousy little dog with her. If a star gave her a lovely story, she always cried. If a star refused to give her good copy, she always peed. You always had water on either occasion." Another fan magazine writer, signing himself "Anonymous" for an article in *American Mercury* in 1943, said of himself, "We have no illusions about our readers. We dish out gossip just short of slander and sticky romance in great gobs ... we attribute lowbrow profundities to actors who have never been within hailing distance of an idea. We glorify clotheshorses, most of whom we despise and all of whom we envy."

By the beginning of the thirties, fans could purchase nearly two dozen monthly fan magazines, most of them poorly edited and wholly unreliable. But then, "reliable" is a relative term. With the competition for pictures and stories intensifying almost daily, no one was beyond fudging the truth a little to make their version of the story bigger and juicier. And the studios (and often the stars themselves) collaborated, knowing that any publicity was good publicity for the movie-mad public.

Hollywood had to wait until 1930 to have its own trade publication, *The Hollywood Reporter. The Hollywood Reporter* stands slightly oblique to the heritage of tattletale tabloids, for it was not quite a gossip magazine nor was it a newspaper, although it liked to fancy itself as the latter. Founded by Billy Wilkerson, a former nickelodeon manager and advertising salesman, *The Hollywood Reporter* was the first and by far the most powerful daily newspaper in Hollywood. Of course, beyond a twenty-mile radius, nobody knew the *Reporter* from the *Podunk Press.* But Wilkerson's pages were filled with who's available, who's not, who's in, who's out—the bread and butter of casting directors, producers-to-be, agents on the prowl, and just about anyone else in town. The pages of *The Hollywood Reporter* could make or break a career; it was the New Testament of Tinseltown.

The *Reporter* was always bursting with news. A regular feature, "Hollywood on the Half-Shell," mimicked the style of the gossip columns but opted for a slightly (only slightly) more businesslike tone. Nightclub openings, marriages and divorces, deaths and births were all dutifully chronicled. Feature articles were ghostwritten "tributes" or human-interest stories, such as director George Cukor's valentine to Katharine Hepburn or Jimmy Durante's complaint "No More Women!" A page or more might be filled with a combination of nuptial news and self-promoting blurbs. Wilkerson's headquarters themselves were a bit of Hollywood-style hoopla, with their own haberdashery and barber shop, and marble fireplaces on every floor. Fireplaces in Los Angeles? *The Hollywood Reporter* strove for legitimacy. This in itself was admirable, but the overall effect on the rise and fall of box office receipts was indirect and immeasurable. For direct and measurable results, the studio bosses, and their bosses in New York, as well as every star and starlet from Times Square to Sunset Boulevard, turned to the columns.

*L*ouella Parsons gets on board. Parsons was never as well-turned out or as socially prominent as her rival, Hedda Hopper, but with the unwavering support of Louis B. Mayer at MGM and William Randolph Hearst and his chain of newspapers, she never lacked clout. Photography courtesy of Photofest, New York.

Nowadays, television has made us all instant and savvy consumers of popular culture. Images are everywhere. Years of constant exposure to advertising and the resultant inculcated cynicism have blunted our senses. But in the thirties and forties, sources of information were tightly conscripted, and news was, if not believed absolutely, at least considered generally truthful. In that world, the power and effect of the columnists cannot be overemphasized.

Most American cities had two newspapers, and many had several more than that. Nearly everyone owned a radio and many households tuned it in day and night. Not only entertainment, but business, sports, and politics were discussed daily by prominent columnists like Walter Winchell, Walter Lippman, Westbrook Pegler, Heywood Broun, Mark Sullivan, and Franklin P. Adams. These men (and at first, they were only men) established the tone for public discourse and helped create a charged atmosphere of opinion, where people could feel free to speak on any topic and engage their coworkers, family, and friends in conversation with zeal and assurance. In other words, the mechanism for massive publicity was in place, and Hollywood was ripe to exploit it.

But there was no doubt who the queens of exploitation were: Louella Parsons of the *San Francisco Examiner* and Hedda Hopper of the *Los Angeles Times.* For approximately thirty years, from the advent of sound to the death of Louis B. Mayer in 1956, Parsons and Hopper defined Hollywood, not only to the world, but to itself. Their breathless writing style, their innocent innuendoes, and their half-serious, self-referential wars perfectly encapsulated the era.

Louella Parsons began her career as a movie columnist for the *Chicago Record Herald* in 1918. (She claimed to be the world's first movie columnist, a distinction nobody ever tried to challenge). Parsons moved to New York in the twenties, where she had a popular radio show called *The Hollywood Hotel.* It was her syrupy support of Marion Davies, Hearst's mistress, that brought her to the publishing magnate's attention and subsequently to California.

Needless to say, her association with Hearst brought Louella Parsons a lot of friends and a nearly equal number of foes. When she liked a star, she could turn out effusive, if slightly off-kilter prose ("Joan Crawford is brilliant and as many-faceted as a diamond...a beautiful package of skin, bones, and character"). But if you crossed the Chief, as Parsons like to call Hearst, you crossed the line. After *Citizen Kane* (RKO, 1941), Parsons called Orson Welles "a mean bully" and said, "The boy genius certainly used all his talents just to do a hatchet job."

Parsons' combination of plain English and provocative innuendo proved to be a very successful formula. She describes her scooping of the story of Ingrid Bergman's illegitimate baby as if it holds the import and intrigue of a national crisis. She refers to her contact as "a man of great importance not only in Hollywood, but throughout the United States," and tells of the late-night telephone call in which he whispered, "Louella, Ingrid is going to have a baby." Parsons then engages herself in a moral debate about the value of the story versus the repercussions to her career should the story turn out to be untrue. Then, of course, she runs the story.

Parsons' need to be seen at the center of power (particularly powerful men) would sometimes bubble over into complete sycophancy. When Howard Hughes had just bought RKO studios and was attempting to become a major player in Hollywood, he wooed Parsons, and Parsons went along for the ride, despite the warning bells that went off in her head. She reports Hughes' habit of dropping into an all-night cafe on the fringe of Los Angeles and commandeering the pay phone for hours on end, or calling her at four A.M. and asking her how she's doing. She uses the classic technique of quoting other people's opinions and then denying that she shares them, in order to describe Hughes as a combination of Dracula, Bluebeard, and Satan.

At the height of her fame, the studios jointly (and studios never did anything jointly) contributed the funds to build a private screening room in her Beverly Hills home. In 1944, to celebrate Parsons' twenty-seventh anniversary with the *Examiner,* Hearst held a dinner in her honor which was well-attended by company executives, movie stars, and even the Governor of California, Earl Warren. Jimmy McHugh was asked to write a song for her, of which she dutifully reprinted the lyrics in her memoirs:

Louella, Louella, Louella
Everyone loves you
Louella, Louella, Louella

A magnum of champagne and a lot of half-empty glasses help keep archrivals Hedda Hopper (left) and Louella Parsons from getting too close to each other at this Hollywood cocktail party. *Photograph courtesy of Photofest, New York.*

*H*edda Hopper in her NBC radio days, circa 1940. The powerful columnists ruled Hollywood from the radio airwaves as well as the pages of the press. Here we catch Miss Hopper in an uncharac-teristically modest and fashionable hat. Photography courtesy of Photofest, New York.

What can a fella do?
Press agents go for your column
Oh, how they really love you
Louella, Louella, Louella
And your 1200 newspapers, too.

By the early sixties, with the industry in tatters and the competition from television intensifying, Parsons turned into a conservative hack, complaining to her dwindling audience of readers about the terrors of the modern world. She raged about the "filth" being turned out in Hollywood, claiming that the finest talent in the business was devoting its time to producing films about "cannibalism, homosexuality, incest, infidelity, shocking juvenile delinquency, racial intolerance, and contempt for law and lawmakers."

Hedda Hopper became famous primarily because she accepted the role of Parsons' foil. There was never really any doubt that Parsons held the clout, largely due to her unceasing loyalty to her boss, William Randolph Hearst. Hopper's job, which she seemed to accept with gleeful relish, was to scoop and/or contradict Parsons at every possible turn. Hopper was a failed actress (her real name was Elda Furry) until she stumbled upon the gimmick of the funny hats, which became her trademark. She never learned to type and liked to pick fights—among her long string of enemies were Joan Bennett (who had her chauffeur deliver a live skunk to Hopper's home) and Louis B. Mayer, who gave her her first scoop.

In her own book (written with James Brough), *The Whole Truth and Nothing But,* Hopper chronicles her fancies and her feuds in grand detail. When she admired a star, she could sound like Florence Nightingale. She liked Judy Garland, noting how "at every performance—at concerts, on television, in her new pictures—she has the power to stir an audience to the depths of their hearts, like an old-fashioned revival meeting. 'We have all come through the fire together,' she seems to say, 'and none of us are getting any younger, but we're here together, and I'll love you if you love me.'" When Hopper catches Garland later in her career in concert at Carnegie Hall, she breathlessly exclaims, "The night was one of the most amazing things I ever witnessed. Her fans screamed and applauded after every number. She gave encore after encore, and promised: 'I'll stay all night if you want me.' She threw her head back and used the mike like a trumpet."

But when Hedda Hopper crossed you off her list, you stayed crossed off. Of course, she reserved a very special place in hell for Louella Parsons. When her column began to hit, Hopper gleefully recounted Parsons' up-coast maneuvers. She mocked Parsons' "intelligence service," which included telegraph operators, telephone switchboard girls, beauty parlor assistants, hotel busboys, doctors' and dentists' receptionists—despite the fact that she herself used the same people. She referred to Parsons' husband, Dr. Harry Watson Martin, as Docky-Wocky and Lolly's Pop.

There were other well-known columnists, of course. Adele Rogers St. Johns was the self-styled "Mother Confessor of Hollywood." She began her career as a screenwriter but ended up as a sweet, slightly reactionary grande dame who complained about "the insipidity of the stars of the seventies, where the leading feminine star is the personification of the age's uglification and the male version is as virile as a rained-on bee." There was Florabel Muir, Hollywood correspondent for New York's *Daily News,* who won herself a bulletproof corset from her editor when she was shot in the buttocks during a gangland shootout on Sunset Boulevard. Later came Sheilah Graham, whose prime source of information was her bodybuilder husband, Stanislaus Wotjkiewicz, affectionately know as Bow Wow, who proudly informed Graham's paper, "I've been to three movies in my life. I wouldn't know Mickey Mouse from Gary Cooper."

Hollywood was not the beat of choice for some of the most famous and powerful columnists of the thirties and forties. Walter Winchell, who spent his entire career in New York, started off by covering parties and fights. As the power and influence of the motion picture industry grew, Winchell increasingly sought access to the biggest stars. Winchell could be a bit of a bully, and any stars or starlets who didn't "make nice" to him would find themselves "blind-itemed" the next morning. (A "blind-item," in gossip-column language, is a rumor of inappropriate behavior, unattributed and with names coyly omitted—e.g., "What sullen redhead currently starring in a Warner Bros. weeper was spotted dashing into Lindy's last night looking tipsy?"

*S*heilah Graham surrounded by the tools of her trade—a telephone, a typewriter, and a fountain pen. As the Golden Age waned, the playing field for gossip columnists leveled a bit, allowing her mild-mannered and genial personality to flourish. *Photography courtesy of Photofest, New York.*

Silver Screen

July

15c

Maureen
O'Hara

BUY YOUR 7th WAR LOAN BONDS AT YOUR
FAVORITE MOTION PICTURE THEATRE

*S*ell, sell, sell ... the cover of an issue of Silver Screen *from July 1945 entices its (mostly female) readership to buy tickets to RKO's* The Spanish Main, *to buy war bonds, and—not incidentally— to buy all the fabric, makeup, and accessories they'll need to make themselves appear as devilishly angelic as Maureen O'Hara. Photograph courtesy of Photofest, New York.*

Ed Sullivan, who became a household name in the fifties and sixties due to his enormously popular television show, was, throughout the Golden Age of Hollywood, "The Toast of the Town"—which was the title of a radio show on which he routinely plugged his favorite movies and film stars. He prided himself on calling the shots for a huge chunk of New York's social life and on always knowing where the hottest parties and the most "in" clubs were. For an actor of any standing whatsoever, no trip to New York was considered a publicity success without an evening on the town with Mr. Sullivan and a mention in his column or on his show.

Gossip could be useful in promoting a career, but it could be equally useful in destroying one. The lure of scandal always bubbled below the surface of the gossip columnist's flighty prose—and sometimes not even below it. In the twenties, gossip about the all-too-real problems of Olive Thomas, Wallace Reid, and Fatty Arbuckle (drugs and liquor) sold millions of papers and brought a hearty, if hypocritical, burst of morality to Tinseltown in the form of the Production Code and its blatant self-censorship. Throughout the thirties and into the forties, strict enforcement of the Code left movie sex and violence to the viewer's imagination. In the fifties, magazines like *Confidential* began to go far beyond the previous limits of propriety, reporting real stories of adultery, destructive behavior, and immoral activities both past and present. *Confidential*'s circulation rose above five million in 1957, until a libel suit drove it out of business.

Confidential makes an interesting postscript to the sometimes sordid business of gossip in Hollywood, because its stories were generally true and its language so brazen. After years of cute whispering and tacit ground rules which fed the pablum that ended up in the *The Saturday Evening Post, Reader's Digest,* and *Ladies' Home Journal,* here was a tabloid which, in its own hokey belief in itself, epitomized everything that made the Hollywood publicity circuit the carnival that it was.

With headlines like "Dan Dailey in Drag" and "Rory Calhoun...Still a Convict," *Confidential* was not for polite reading in the parlor. Stories would pour in through the least likely (and most authoritative) channels. Moving companies would report property dispositions in cases of broken homes or ugly separations. Collection agencies would sell information about a has-been who went bankrupt. Sales clerks would report on the gift-buying habits of their favorite stars. Call girls were frequently paid twice—once by their hopefully anonymous date and then again, more grandly, out of one of *Confidential*'s accounts.

The studios, for a while, played the game. Stories would be "traded" as a way to keep key contract stars in line. When someone at *Confidential* got the goods on Columbia boss Harry Cohn, one of Cohn's emissaries quickly peddled the magazine a bit of dirt on Kim Novak in exchange. Harry came out smelling like a rose, and Miss Novak quickly learned the price of stardom.

It was all a very closed shop, and a cozy world. Paul Macnamara, who was David O. Selznick's press agent, put it plainly: "Every top exec, from all the studios, every actor and actress, every director and writer, every bit player and extra, and of course every agent had read every word of every column by lunch time." The press agents would hire spies such as bellhops and waiters, with instructions to call them with any news of their clients. This "news" would then be dutifully doled out to whichever columnist was in favor that week.

Sometimes the work of a gossip columnist resembled nothing so much as a chapter from an Ian Fleming novel. Parsons worked the Cannes Film Festival, catching parties and screenings while her assistant toiled away in a soundproofed hotel room, one hand on the telephone. After each story was typed and sent to the wire reporters by courier, Parsons would amble by to collect the used carbon papers. "There were no secrets in Cannes," Parsons reported. "The bellboys, clerks, waiters, chambermaids, and other members of the hotel staff were all in the pay of the newspaper and magazine correspondents from all over the world. They steamed open letters, eavesdropped on conversations, listened in on phone calls, and scavenged in waste baskets."

A special place in the world of the Hollywood writers must be reserved for the great Ezra Goodman, whose wicked chronicle of his years as a columnist, *The Fifty-Year Decline and Fall of Hollywood,* provides very entertaining ballast to all the sickeningly sweet prose and hypercritical vitriol that Rogers, Parsons, Hopper, et al. spewed out. Goodman did it all, from being a press agent to newspaper reporting, from Manhattan to the Mexican border. All the time, he displayed a sharp wit and a healthy delight in wading through the bull. He'd mock the moguls for their imperiousness ("Darryl Zanuck harbored a grievance against me for years for alluding to his 'fuzzy mustache'") and profiled the forgotten folks who held the town's rumor mill together. Goodman interviewed Whitey Hendry, MGM's Chief of Police, who was the first man on the scene when Paul Bern, Jean Harlow's husband, killed himself, scooping the LA police by a clear forty minutes.

One of Goodman's most amusing anecdotes entails his detailed chronicle of the Hollywood gift-giving caste system, a sociological document that gives us a clear glimpse of the relative power of the gossip columnists. Apparently, all the leading Hollywood producers pooled their Christmas lists and divided up the names into A, B, and C lists. The C's were nobodies from unheard-of papers who obediently followed their press book formulas—they'd get a box of handkerchiefs or a dinky toy. The B's were too important to insult, but not important enough to flatter, and would come out from under their tree with a piece of ostentatious jewelry or a leather billfold. Only the A crowd—the names, the ones who could make or break a picture—received true largesse: a new car or a truckload of toys donated in their name to a home for orphans.

It was Ezra Goodman who institutionalized the legend of Louis B. Mayer's chicken soup. It seems that out of respect for his dear, departed mother, Mayer devised a particularly chunky brand of chicken soup to be served in his private dining room. Eventually the recipe was passed on to the studio commissary, whereupon Mayer ordered that it be served every day for thirty-five cents a bowl. Like all good stories, this one is fundamentally untrue. But it "sells" the image of the wonderful, nurturing studio, run by a caring, paternal boss.

Great writer that he was, Goodman knew that it was the story, not the truth, that counted. And so he ends his chronicle of life as a Hollywood columnist by saying goodbye "not to Louis B. Mayer, but to Louis B. Mayer's chicken soup." ★

Window display for Desiree (Fox, 1954). This elegant and anonymous department store exploited the motion picture to market their its own line of hats, "inspired by the motion picture." *Photograph courtesy of Photofest, New York.*

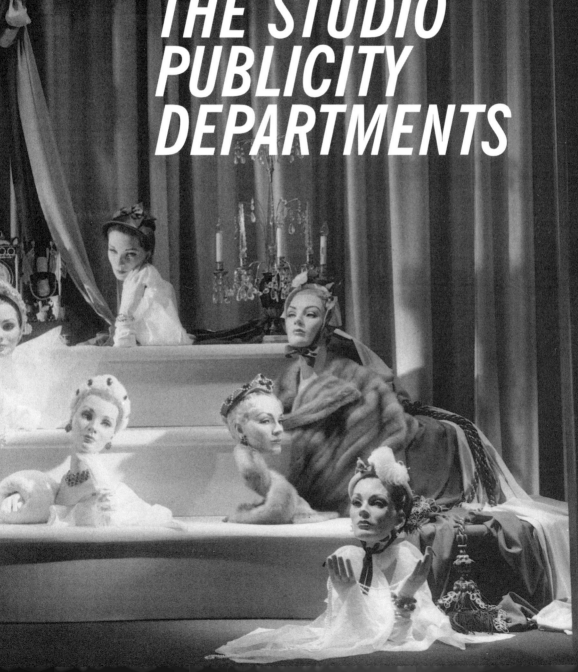

Chapter 5
PLANTING AND PLUGGING: THE STUDIO PUBLICITY DEPARTMENTS

"**B**esides sex," wrote anthropologist Hortense Powdermaker in 1950, "publicity—good or bad, free or paid for, false or true—is regarded as an essential ingredient" of success. Time has proven this Hollywood dictum to be true—anyone would do anything to get noticed. What is generally unappreciated is how efficiently and aggressively the industry exploited this angle, and how overwhelmingly successful this exploitation proved to be.

All the major motion picture studios organized their departments in the most rigorous manner, with strong lines of command and strict definitions of responsibility—and publicity was no different. The publicity department had one person who set the tone of the entire operation, and the flow of power was downward from there. Everyone knew what his or her job was—to get pictures of the studio's stars in the papers and their names in the news, to make certain the stories and photographs were always flattering and in keeping with the stars' public image and stature, and to assure that the studio's current feature films were mentioned in every paragraph.

The methods that were employed to accomplish these goals were as varied as the number of people who tried them. In the course of her research in Hollywood in the late forties (a particularly desperate time in the business), Powdermaker noted several of the most notorious ploys: spreading rumors, creating false organizations and awards, building up guest lists to important parties, and engineering competitions. In the most general way, this unique blend of unrestrained business practices and a prurient appeal to people's interest in wealth, sex, and fame underlay all publicists' work.

At times, relations between the studio publicity departments and the working press resembled a tumultuous marriage—kisses one day, brickbats the next. Columnist Ezra Goodman recounts the travails of Benjamin R. Crisler, the *New York Times'* second-string movie reviewer. Crisler's negative review of a mild Goldwyn musical called *They Shall Have Music* (1939), starring Jascha Heifetz, was personally pulled from the late edition by no less an eminence than Arthur Sulzberger himself, the paper's publisher. Sulzberger ordered the then number-three man Bosley Crowther to rewrite it. What was the motivation behind this apparent subterfuge? Apparently, Goldwyn had pegged *They Shall Have*

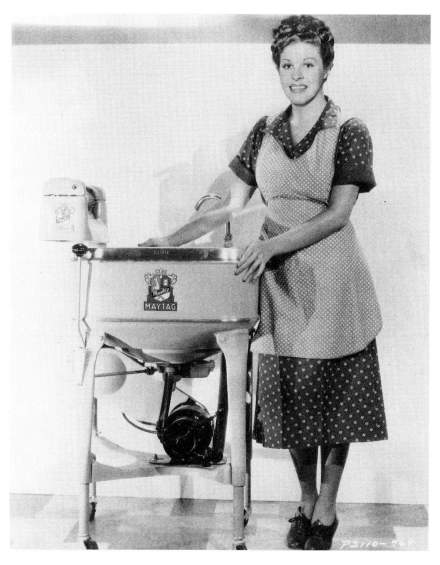

*M*artha Raye helps to sell Maytag washing machines. Paramount would never ask one of its glamorous stars, such as Claudette Colbert, to pose in an apron next to an ordinary domestic appliance, but a comic actress like Martha Raye made a perfect spokesperson for a machine designed to lighten the drudgery of housework. Photograph courtesy of Photofest, New York.

Music as a major picture, and Sulzberger's access to the powerful image-makers in Hollywood was not about to be adversely affected by a lowly critic. Crisler learned his lesson; he later told Goodman, "if you start off your review by saying it was 'sumptuous,' even if it was lousy," no one at the top will take offense.

Poor Mr. Crisler was not singled out. Goodman recalls regular threats from Harry Brandt, the head of publicity at Paramount, and Charles Skouras, ditto at Twentieth Century-Fox (and the studio head's brother). The studios decided amongst themselves which members of the press qualified for accreditation and which did not. After Edwin Schallert of the *Los Angeles Times* retired, he and his wife had to plead for seats at previews, and after Harry Crocker of the *Los Angeles Examiner* died, his paper had to drum up mourners for his funeral. Meanwhile, favored faces could write their own passes. Edith Gwynne married Billy Wilkerson (publisher of *The Hollywood Reporter)* and was in everyone's good graces to the end of her days.

The studios would spend fortunes trying to control the press—and they were willing to lose fortunes, if necessary. When Frank Nugent of the *New York Times* panned Fox's *The Story of Alexander Graham Bell* (1939), the studio withdrew all of its *Times* ads for one year. Later, Darryl Zanuck, the man who ordered the ads pulled, hired Nugent to write screenplays. Charles Einfeld, who ran the Warner Bros. publicity department, laid pressure on the bosses of Otis Guernsey *(New York Herald-Tribune)* and Archer Winsten *(New York Post)* in an eventually unsuccessful effort to soften their reviews of his company's pictures. When the critic Grace Kingsley of the *Los Angeles Times* was in disfavor, one theater manager took to flashing a sign on the screen between shows that said, "Grace Kingsley thinks this is a bad picture. What do you think?" Within a week, Kingsley's friends from the *Times* had returned to the theater. When the sign flashed on the screen, they stood up; chanted, "We think Grace Kingsley is right"; and walked out.

Ezra Goodman is particularly gleeful in his recounting of tales from inside the publicity departments. Billy Grady, MGM's casting director, told Goodman about the time that department chief Howard Strickling scolded him for telling an interviewer he had discovered James Stewart and Van Johnson. Even though Grady was right, Strickling had to remind him that only Louis B. Mayer could be publicly credited with the discovery of a star. Goodman also notes that bad reviews could easily be circumvented by pressure placed upon newspaper advertising departments. It seems that a picture's score on a newspaper's "movie meter" (a version of the one- to four-star rating system) could miraculously change overnight. "Since many readers never go beyond glancing at the meter," Goodman writes, "this was a tactic often used by movie press agents and advertisers to tone down the effect of a negative review." Eventually the studios learned how to make even bad reviews work. When *White Zombie* (United Artists, 1932) debuted at the Rivoli in Manhattan and was butchered by the critics, the studio ran ads quoting the reviews and added the caption "when the critics' noses went up, the box office receipts went up as well."

No one had a bigger or better publicity operation than Metro-Goldwyn-Mayer. As befitted its role as the gold-plated studio of the era, Howard Strickling's staff turned the business of motion picture publicity into a campaign as complex, widespread, and unavoidable as a military invasion. This invasion proceeded along several fronts—personal appearances by the stars, color and black-and-white posters, trailers, recordings of the theme songs, and newspaper and radio advertisements, as well as product endorsements, book tie-ins, giveaways, and contests. Each MGM exhibitor received a data book that listed the names and addresses for each "exchange"—the office where the film, posters, and all related materials could be picked up and dropped off—as well as the names and circulation figures of all the newspapers and magazines accepting MGM ads, sources for radio (and, later, TV) announcements, transcribed interviews, sheet music, and press releases.

MGM's financial resources far outstripped those of all its rivals. For the other studios, especially the constantly struggling Warner Bros. and Columbia, the heart of the publicity department's work was the press book. Today the press books offer a fascinating glimpse into the social habits and sexual mores of the thirties and forties. Press books were created for the exhibitors' eyes only, and the goal was craven manipulation. Here the not-so-subtle machinations of the studio publicity departments are plain to see, laid bare in a manner that was almost always hidden from public view.

*W*indow display to promote Gun Fury (Columbia, 1953). An inventive window-dresser for the Foster & Avery department store in Portland, Maine, utilized his stock to tie in with a studio-supported coloring contest, offering a very complete cowboy outfit to the lucky boy who could sit all the way through the movie. *Photograph courtesy of Photofest, New York.*

Every studio, from giant MGM to tiny Republic, used press books. Every feature film, both A's and B's, had one. From the middle of the silent era up to just before the collapse of the studio system, a total of approximately three thousand press books were assembled, printed, and distributed. More than half of these books are still extant, carefully preserved in major research libraries. A peek into their contents offers a glimpse into a hidden piece of motion picture history.

The typical press book ran somewhere between twenty and thirty pages. Each would begin with a display of the different advertisements and posters available to the exhibitor to place in the theater window or lobby and in the local papers. This section would be followed by a page or two of promotional ideas specifically tailored to the movie in question. Near the end, the book would include a cast list, a synopsis of the plot, several "prewritten" reviews (to give to papers and radio stations who couldn't afford their own critics), and promotional portraits of the stars.

Different types of films demanded different kinds of press books. Action and adventure films were usually top-heavy with graphics— images of the star (usually a man) on the move, with the title or a buzz-phrase exploding in the background. For *Captain Blood* (1935), Warner Bros. included two pages of pirate tie-ins (bags of sand with "gold" pieces on top, pirate costumes for boys, spyglasses, and a model pirate ship to rig up in the lobby), as well as a suggestion for a local promotional angle that would involve your local fencing team. There was an address for ordering multiple copies of Raphael Sabatini's novel (with a picture of Errol Flynn on the cover, of course) and a page of photographs of fashionably dashing men's ties, jackets, pipes, suits, and suspenders, available in bulk from manufacturers across the nation for table-top display at your local haberdasher. Women were not completely forgotten: the press book also offered the damsel in distress customized brush and comb sets, skin lotions, perfume, and a snazzy "buccaneer" dress modeled by Olivia de Havilland. For *Gun Fury* (1953), Columbia set up its distributors with posters, lobby cards, and framed stills which were distributed to local Western apparel dealers to augment their stock.

Warner Bros.' press book for *The Big Sleep* (1946) was similarly male-aggressive. Included on the largest poster was the warning: "Baby, you asked for action, and you're gonna get some!" Several of the smaller posters featured equally forceful, if somewhat illiterate, messages: "Their kind of love-madness! Their kind of madly exciting smash!," "A story as violent as their love," "Teeming with star-team excitement!" The distributor was the appropriately named Dominant Pictures Corporation. Still photographs of star Humphrey Bogart and director Howard Hawks completed the hard sell, and throwing in Lauren Bacall at her loveliest did not hurt.

Further down the prestige ladder, things got even pushier. For the B feature *Calling Philo Vance* (Warner Bros., 1932), the press book suggested loading your lobby with hidden clues based upon the movie's plot—these included a lipstick case, a fireplace poker, and a blood-stained airplane model. It also suggested that you try to hire a local police officer to come play the titular detective, or that you convince a bellhop to go through a local hotel lobby crying "Calling Philo Vance!" No consideration was given to how these ideas might adversely affect local law enforcement or the peace and quiet of the hotel guests. Of course, S.S. Van Dine's novel was available in bulk (with promises of a generous profit attached). An entire lobby display was available, consisting of posters, facsimile props, and merchandise tie-ins. As a last resort, desperate exhibitors were advised to place a wool Scottish terrier (after the dog in the movie, Captain MacTavish) on a table in the lobby and place a recording of the dog promoting the picture on a concealed record player underneath it. (Neither dog, recording, nor player was provided.) For *Road Show* (Warner Bros., 1941), the studio invented a bizarre psychoanalytic game involving "ludicralunes" and "sophistalunes" for theatergoers.

The Treasure of the Sierra Madre (Warner Bros., 1948) was marketed specifically to appeal to father-son theater outings. The press book included a jigsaw puzzle contest, a treasure hunt, and matching men's and boy's Marlboro sports shirts. There was also a tie-in to the book, issued in a large, illustrated format designed to appeal to children, plus a bizarre Mexican travel tie-in. ("Note: if there's an official representative of the Mexican Government in your town, get down and see him pronto.") The fact that the movie featured its own father-son combo (director John Huston and his father, actor Walter Huston) was probably coincidental.

In many cases, the press books made a strong pitch to the

A page from the Warner Bros. press book for Road Show (1941). This Hal Roach comedy, starring John Hubbard and Carole Landis, revealed signs of desperation with the offer of a free "humor analysis quiz." Future generations of moviegoers may be forgiven for wondering who was the real "ludicralune" here. Photograph courtesy of the Wisconsin Center for Film and Theater Research, Madison, Wisconsin.

*S*heet music in the window of McCrory's Department Store, Philadelphia, 1930. Before the widespread popularity of the phonograph record, sheet music was the only way for songs to be heard. In order to differentiate their product from the millions of others and attract the attention of the public, publishers would decorate their covers with colorful photographs of the stars of stage and screen. *Photograph courtesy of Photofest, New York.*

exhibitors to appeal to women. Women were perceived as the largest part of the moviegoing audience and also the member of the household who was in charge of selecting which picture to see. The stories of so-called "women's pictures" featured domestic dramas and starred willful, if flawed, female leads. Warner Bros. was the master of this genre, and Bette Davis was their star nonpareil. The studio press books for *Jezebel* (1938) and *Dark Victory* (1939) are social documents of the highest order, and vastly entertaining to boot. Considering the reception and reputation of the films they were advertising, they were wildly successful as well.

The *Dark Victory* press book is virtually a Bette Davis museum. The prewritten reviews are geared entirely to descriptions of her performance, including quotes from the character in the movie and from Miss Davis herself (the latter most likely fabricated by the publicity department). The posters—and there were twenty to choose from—consisted primarily of gigantic blowups of Davis' severely-coiffed head. The press book advertised an eleven-chapter serial, "The Life Story of Bette Davis," available for syndication from the *Boston American.*

Direct appeals were made to women who wished to emulate Miss Davis. Orry-Kelly's ensembles, created for the star, were available off the rack from your local retailer. The featured item was a spring suit trimmed in silver fox and sable, with a sable muff, certainly beyond the budget of nearly every patron. Full-page advertisements, prominently featuring Davis' photograph, were laid out for insertion into *Redbook, Life, Good Housekeeping,* and a dozen more general-interest magazines. Davis herself offered an entire page of makeup tips, and the studio offered a bedroom suite, modeled after the one used in the movie, available from the Pendleton Furniture Company.

For *Jezebel,* Warner Bros. offered a Jezebel hat (black straw with a velvet ribbon and pink roses), a Jezebel hairdo, and recipes for a Jezebel cocktail and Jezebel-style Southern fried chicken. The theme song from the movie, performed by Guy Lombardo, was available on disc from your local record dealer or in the form of sheet music from the publisher, Harms, in New York. Interestingly enough, despite the overwhelming presence of Davis' portrait in the vicinity of so much selling, the press book goes to great lengths to protect their star's reputation. "Bette Davis' name or photograph," they say, "must not be used for any commercial tie-up in any way whatsoever." Except by the studio, of course. These sorts of activities didn't seem to bother co-star George Brent at all, whose likeness is seen in the press book gladly holding a Packard Lekto-Shaver and using Calox Toothpowder.

The exploitation of personality didn't particularly upset Joan Crawford, either. She customarily went out well ahead of the studio publicity people and sold herself in the flesh. The press book for *Mildred Pierce* (Warner Bros., 1945) is full of the kind of dangerous-female warnings that Crawford probably begged for: "Please don't tell anyone what she did," "Loving her was like shaking hands with the Devil." Strangely, the book is devoid of fashion advice, interviews, or advertisements. Apparently Miss Crawford preferred to take care of such things herself, and her contract specifically allowed for it.

Pictures less driven by big stars resorted to all kinds of exploitation to attract exhibitors'—and consequently moviegoers'—attention. The press book for *Johnny Belinda* (Warner Bros., 1948) included lead Jane Wyman posing with Chesterfield cigarettes, Lux soap, Lipton teabags, and platters of Rogers silver plate. Patrons were offered Johnny Belinda haircuts, fall outfits, and dinner gowns. For *Dangerous Female* (Warner Bros., 1931), starring Ricardo Cortez and Bebe Daniels, Lux soap made another appearance, along with Bebe Daniels postcards, but the film had much greater success when it was redone a few years later with the title *The Maltese Falcon. Desiree* (Fox, 1954) inspired a craze for flamboyant Empire-style hats. For *The Scarf* (1951), United Artists offered the title neckwear in a variety of colors, despite the fact that the press books featured, on the same page, a publicity photograph of John Ireland attempting to strangle Mercedes McCambridge with it. Apparently even murder weapons were regarded as fair game for exploitation and promotion.

Another niche that the press books were adept at exploiting was the so-called "ethnic" film. The major studios never did much in the way of cultivating their Black, Jewish, Asian, and Hispanic audiences on a national level, partially because those audiences weren't large enough to support the level of investment that the A pictures needed, but also, unfortunately, because they feared backlash from racist and xenophobic

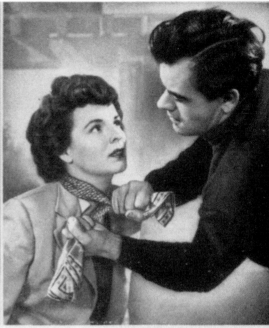

How to Wear and Tie Them

A colorful print scarf is standard equipment in every woman's wardrobe, for it is one of the most adaptable articles of clothing. It's good for keeping milady's neck warm in the winter, but it's even better an accessory to dress up a suit or tailored dress. Shown here are five ways to wear a scarf, four with dresses and one with suit.

Miss Ann Silver, Glentex scarf style expert, suggests these novel scarf ideas:

Dramatize your traditional black dress with a bold, bright accent by using identical scarfs as belt and collar, made by tying simple knot (*top left*);

Provide a beautiful variation for basic dress or suit by fashioning lustrous satin scarf into a bolero blouse, done by folding under one corner and tying ends around neck, making revers of left and right corners and folding under bottom corner and tying around waist (*bottom left*);

A classic sports dress is transformed by using the scarf in a loose drape, tying one corner around neck, letting the rest fall naturally and spreading at the waist under tight belt (*top center*);

Lend that Paris-fashion oblique look to a simple tailored dress by tying loosely at neck, draping one corner over shoulder and drawing other corner to waist (*bottom right*).

An additional idea is to use the scarf as a choker (*top right*), demonstrated on Academy Award winner Mercedes McCambridge. John Ireland, her co-star in "The Scarf," I. G. Goldsmith's powerful drama of violent passions opening   at the   Theater through United Artists' release.

Mr. Ireland folds scarf neatly, places it around Miss McCambridge's neck, grasps it tightly in both fists and pulls as hard as he can. The effect is positively breath-taking!

A page from the United Artists' press book for The Scarf (1951). John Ireland and Mercedes McCambridge starred in this standard lunatic-on-the-loose murder mystery. Here, Miss McCambridge obligingly models the murder weapon, to the point of allowing the murderer to adjust the knot. *Photograph courtesy of the* Wisconsin Center for Film and Theater Research, Madison, Wisconsin.

A dog team leads Ann Blyth to her latest premiere. As a publicity stunt for The World in His Arms (Universal, 1952), the studio sent Blyth to Anchorage, Alaska. This picture was taken at 8:00 P.M. on June 20, the longest day of the year, under the clear light of the midnight sun. The star was sledding her way to the Fourth Avenue Theatre after entertaining troops at the Elmendorf Air Force Base and Fort Richardson. Photograph courtesy of Photofest, New York.

exhibitors in the Midwest and the South. But the press books could be tailored to specific needs, and this offered some studios the opportunity to market to minorities. The very fact that most studio-owned theaters were located in the centers of big cities, where the greatest number of ethnic minorities lived, worked, and entertained themselves, was incentive enough to develop stars and stories which appealed to them. But these considerations were balanced by very strong social forces which opposed the now nearly universally accepted idea that Black, Jewish, Asian, and Hispanic men and women had stories to tell which were as compelling as anyone else's.

For a while, Fanny Brice was being developed for stardom. The press book for *Be Yourself* (United Artists, 1930) offered an essay contest, sheet music for the songs Brice sings in the movie, lyric sheets, an order form for lobby accessories, and sample postcards. None of the material mentions Brice's background in the Yiddish theater, masking rather than reinforcing the movie's message of individuality. Monogram Pictures enjoyed great success with its Charlie Chan series, which starred the very western Sidney Toler as the oriental detective but did give a lot of feature work to Asian-American actors. The press books included long, sympathetic profiles of Benson Fong and the black actor Mantan Moreland, and encouraged exhibitors to feature them (with the usual warning: "If your situation demands it, hold a special showing"—for "special," read "segregated").

By 1950, exhibitors were no longer chained to the studios, and the need for the press books had dissolved. Television was rapidly replacing radio as the advertiser's dream medium—one in which the film could, quite logically, advertise itself directly. Daily newspapers were slowly dying on the vine. The trend toward independent production and the rise of the independent star totally obliterated the need for the factory-like studio publicity departments. Each film was built, marketed, and exhibited on its own. Opportunities for uniform presentation and control were gone. Sensational stunts were the order of the day, such as the time that Universal sent poor Ann Blyth to Anchorage, Alaska, to debut *The World in His Arms* (1952) under the midnight sun.

It was at this precarious moment in Hollywood history that producer Mervyn LeRoy decided to publish a serious how-to book on breaking into the film business, called *It Takes More Than Talent.* In his chapter called "The Praisery Department," LeRoy advises the future publicists of America: "Nothing should make their stars look ridiculous. Greer Garson can't appear on the radio show *The Adventures of Maisie* as Maisie; it wouldn't be becoming to her. Irene Dunne can't by-line a story 'I Believe in Divorce.' In the first place, she doesn't. In the second place, the public doesn't want to associate the thought of divorce with Irene Dunne. You don't throw hotcha leg art, suitable for Shelley Winters or Marilyn Monroe, at Margaret Sullavan. You don't show a rugged he-man wearing an apron. Each star has an individual build-up, in keeping with his or her screen personality."

LeRoy continues to explain how the publicist is the middleman, trying to give the reporter what his or her editor wants while trying to protect the star from unfavorable publicity that might damage his or her box-office value. "In public relations," he concluded, "the publicist has to blend the temperament of the star with the temperament of the writer. The star may not feel that a story on how she bakes lamb chops with rosemary is important, but if you're the editor of a cookbook, it's important to you."

There is a valedictorian tone to LeRoy's encouraging pronouncements. It's almost as if he suspects that the world into which he is urging his readers is disappearing when he proclaims that "Your classroom will be the magazine stand; your library the newsstand."

The studio publicity departments may have seen their day come and go, but the hype intensified, nevertheless. New films were tossed out into the market like unexploded bombs, and the next generation of publicists pounced upon them hoping each detonation could be bigger and louder than the one before. The modern era of film exploitation began at the Cannes Film Festival in 1954, when actress Simone Sylva startled Robert Mitchum by taking off her top and posing for an army of photographers in the actor's arms. (Sadly, Miss Sylva's attempts to gain the limelight failed and she committed suicide six months later). The era of the mogul-managed, carefully modulated, and generally morally clean exploitation ended, replaced by the star-driven, wild, titillating era we live in today.

This change is not wholly good or bad, merely emblematic. All the cool calculation of the old studio publicity departments took advantage of the stars and mistreated many of them, a situation difficult to imagine today. The inherent conservatism of a business governed so completely by profit kept out many important messages and excluded a lot of talented people from participating in filmmaking. But it's not easy to argue that the bombshell approach to motion picture promotion which has dominated the industry since the sixties serves the world any better. In place of narrowly defined choices, there are too many; instead of uplift and direction, there is cynicism and pandering—in advertising and presentation as much as in content. And this, it seems, represents a definite loss.

Even behind the evident facade put up by the studio publicity departments in Hollywood's Golden Age, life was often quite good. In 1960, for the Cannes premiere of *Never on Sunday,* United Artists rented the Ambassades nightclub and converted it into a Greek taverna, complete with a live band, souvlaki and feta cheese, and endless bottles of fine Greek wine. The wingding lasted two days, and resulted in hundreds of delirious guests and thousands of broken plates and glasses. Melina Mercouri summed up the event to Cari Beauchamp, the daughter of the founder of the festival. "I'll speak modestly about the film, about my acting, about anything," she said, "… but not about that party." ★

*S*ometimes the blinding flashbulbs and clunky teacups are just too much for a movie star to handle! Jane Wyman (left) and Irene Dunne don full Hollywood drag—shades, hats, pearls, and gloves—for this artfully arranged lunchtime cameo. *Photograph courtesy of Photofest, New York.*

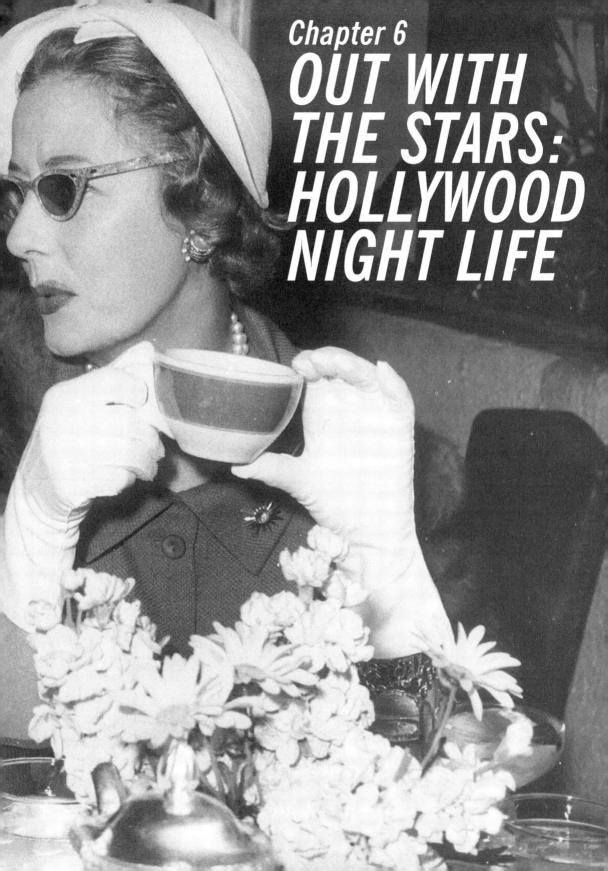

A movie star's work is never done. When the klieg lights shut down for the day, the neon lights of the city beckon. In the Golden Age of Hollywood, being seen at the right place and with the right people was as important to the cultivation of stardom as any publicity photograph or poster.

The structure of social life in Hollywood was complicated; figuring it out was part of the game. Starlets on the rise, accompanied by their agent and a studio photographer, would seek out the most popular nightclubs, dance with the most beloved actors (provided they were contracted to the same studio), and spew quotes to any reporter within a quarter of a mile. Meanwhile, the biggest names would come out at night only when they owed the studio a favor or were jockeying for a raise. The vast majority of actors worked the middle ground. For them, a night on the town was an opportunity to provoke a rivalry, angle for a better part, shill for a sponsor, send up a trial balloon to measure their status, or sprint into someone's flattering flashbulb. Of course, sometimes stars went out just for fun—after three or four Polynesian Firepot cocktails at Trader Vic's, who cared what the *Hollywood Reporter* said?

Hollywood at night was probably the best time to see the stars with their hair down. Away from the glare of the lights and the watchful eyes of their bosses, actors and actresses could occasionally be seen behaving like ordinary—or at least ordinary wealthy—people. Ezra Goodman understood this implicitly. To introduce a chapter called "The Night Life of the Gods" in his book *The Fifty-Year Decline and Fall of Hollywood,* Goodman said, "I have found, as a journalist, that there is often more doing after hours away from the camera than during the working day in front of it. And though these after-hours doings are mostly frivolous, they can often be more revealing about the community than a stack of double-dome tomes authored by psychiatrists, anthropologists, and sociologists on grants from the Rockefeller, Guggenheim and Ford foundations and sponsored by the Museum of Modern Art Film Library and the Academy of Motion Picture Arts and Sciences combined."

Hollywood was not a party town at birth. Until the late twenties, this rambling collection of shacks, back lots, and bungalows was deserted after sundown. Newly hatched millionaires fled to established outposts of civilization like San Francisco or Mexico when they wanted to find an

*T*imes Square at night. Back when it was Longacre Square, the intersection of Broadway and 42nd
Street was an unfashionable residential enclave. By the 1940s, it was home to the biggest movie
palaces and nightclubs in America, and, outside of Hollywood, the largest playpen of the stars.
Photograph courtesy of the Museum of the City of New York, Gottscho-Schleisner Collection, New York.

MGM star Bebe Daniels, her husband, producer Ben Lyon, and their son Richard share dessert at the Brown Derby. The Derby, with its characteristic hat-shaped roof and wall of caricatures, was a favorite watering hole to the movie colony for over fifty years. Photograph courtesy of Photofest, New York.

all-night party or weekend getaway. At the very least, their chauffeurs would drive them all the way out on Sunset Boulevard to Santa Monica, where they could douse their sorrows in the warm waters of the Pacific. But the Depression and the Production Code laid strict limits on this sort of widespread extravagance, and soon everybody wanted to be a homebody. Dining and shopping were the drugs of choice for what passed as the new sobriety in Tinseltown.

The first big burst of Hollywood night life sprang up around the ballroom of the city's top hotel. In 1921, the Cocoanut Grove opened in the Ambassador Hotel, where orchestras led by Phil Harris and Guy Lombardo would entertain the movie royalty until the wee hours. Over the years, Rudy Vallee, Freddy Martin, Ozzie Nelson, and Merv Griffin all took turns walking across the Grove's famous bandstand. The hotel's Fiesta Room was the site of the Academy Awards ceremony from its inception in 1930 until 1935, when it was moved to the rival Biltmore. An ill-fated attempt to modernize the Grove in the late fifties killed whatever class the club had retained, and it finally staggered into bankruptcy in 1989.

Stars looking for the light discovered that being a moving target in the middle of a crowded dance floor did not make for a flattering photograph. The scene soon shifted from the clubs to the restaurants. The cult of the Hollywood restaurant is tricky to explain—after all, everyone has to eat. But there is eating, and then there is "eating." Movie stars never considered restaurants merely places to eat. A career could be made by being seen at the right place, at the right time, and with the right people. The hierarchies which emerged in the dining rooms lining Hollywood and Sunset Boulevards were as rigid and unforgiving as those of any European court, with favored celebrities reserving tables by the window or within viewing range of gossip columnists and photographers.

The first of the big Hollywood "hash houses" was the Brown Derby, which opened directly across the street from the Cocoanut Grove in 1926. The Brown Derby was built in the shape of a gigantic hat, a classic example of the rootless, vernacular architecture that characterizes southern California to this very day. The caricatures which adorned (and eventually covered) its walls were originally bribes offered by the artist Eddie Vitch in exchange for free meals. In 1934, restaurateur Robert

Cobb bought the original Derby and its unhatted sister joint at Hollywood and Vine. He promptly added his signature dish to the menu—chopped iceberg lettuce, bacon strips, hard-boiled eggs, and Roquefort cheese—and gave the world the Cobb Salad.

For choice star-grazing, very few restaurants topped Chasen's, which began life as a tiny diner on Beverly Boulevard in Beverly Hills in 1936. Dave Chasen ran his place like a theater—the best seats were allotted to the in-crowd and waiters in starched uniforms pirouetted across the floor like Fred Astaire. Chasen refused to allow photographers in the restaurant, which of course created a mob of them every night under the awning, many of them placed there by the stars' agents themselves. Chasen liked to pamper his favorites: Orson Welles had a telephone plugged into his booth to facilitate deal-making in the middle of his double order of roast beef, and Howard Hughes always had a private room in which he could take his usual dinner of a triple glass of tomato juice, a green salad, a thin butterflied steak, and coffee.

Chasen's had the atmosphere of a small club. It stayed open until four in the morning—and there was always a show after hours. One night Bert Lahr performed his vaudeville act; another night Ray Bolger pushed two tables together and created a specialty dance on the spot. Chasen himself recounted the time the writers Nunnally Johnson and Charles MacArthur stayed up drinking well past the closing hour. A polite request from the owner for his guests to leave prompted the two drunken scribes to lift Chasen up bodily, toss him out onto the street, lock the door, and continue drinking in peace. The original Chasen's finally ran out of gas in April 1995. A "new" Chasen's opened at another location in 1997, but the real thing is gone forever.

Dave Chasen's only real rival for the title of sandwich-maker to the stars was Prince Michael Romanoff and his self-named restaurant. Romanoff wasn't really a Romanoff, of course—his real name was Harry Gerguson and he was born in Cincinnati or Brooklyn, depending upon whose story you believe. But his act was appreciated by Hollywood's royalty, which, after all, was as fake as he was. Romanoff designed a faux-crest for his House of Romanoff—a cocktail glass crossed with a swizzle stick—and was known to summon his staff to their duty every afternoon by brandishing an alligator-skin riding crop.

*J*anet Leigh and Judy Garland at the Mocambo nightclub, July 1949. Some stars were having too good a time to worry about posed publicity shots. Here Garland and Leigh share some private hilarity over a champagne cocktail and a mug of Irish coffee. *Photograph courtesy of Photofest, New York.*

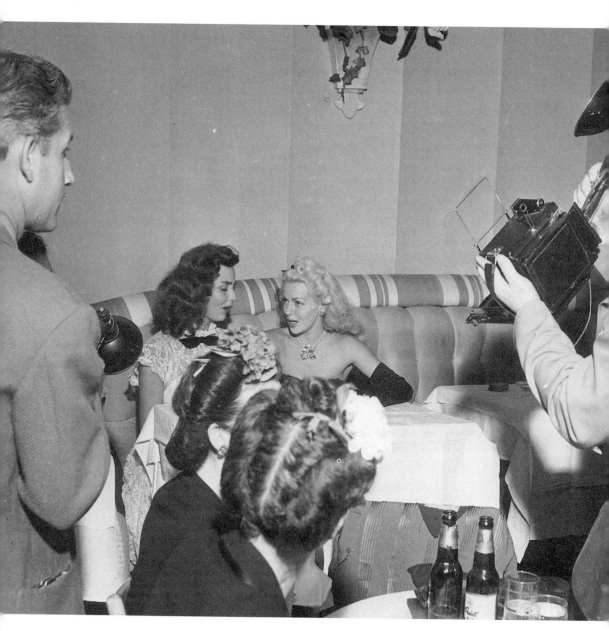

*J*ennifer Jones and Lana Turner at Ciro's, March 1944. A photographer photographs the photographers at a party thrown for Jennifer Jones by David O. Selznick in honor of Jones' winning the
Academy Award for Best Actress in Song of Bernadette (1943). Turner used her proximity to Jones
(plus a dazzling necklace) to assure herself a place in the papers. Photograph courtesy of Photofest, New York.

In its first incarnation at 326 North Rodeo Drive, Romanoff's was highly aristocratic. The first booth was always reserved for Alfred Hitchcock, an honor Romanoff admitted Hitch was given by mistake ("I tried to move him to the side-room, but he hasn't been back since"). The main dining room had only five booths, located to the left of the staircase. After Hitchcock was evicted, they were reserved for Humphrey Bogart, agent Abe Lastfogel, Louis B. Mayer, Darryl Zanuck, and Harry Cohn. When the Prince decamped to 240 South Rodeo Drive in 1951, he installed twenty-eight booths. The Royal Era was ended. Once any schmoe could get a booth, why bother?

Chasen's and Romanoff's were the choice spots to be served, snapped, and squired, but the town was growing. By the end of the forties, there were nearly two dozen clubs and restaurants famous enough to earn their own mentions in the columns and newsreels. Press agents worked day and night (but mostly night) to get their clients seen going in or out of any of them. Perino's, on Wilshire Boulevard, was the place to show off your latest (borrowed) jewels. At Sasha's Palate, diners would eat Roman-style, reclining on couches as waitresses in togas served roasted pheasant, suckling pig, and baby goat. In the Pompeii Room at Ciro's, you could be presented with a Vesuvius cocktail which bubbled over when served.

It was probably in Hollywood that the habit of naming dishes after personalities began. To have a triple-decker sandwich with your name on it was free publicity at its best. In Paramount's commissary, the studio's biggest stars went down very well with Pepsi, according to Pauline Kissinger, head of the Paramount restaurant for several decades. You could start with a Bob Hope cocktail (tomato juice and yogurt with a dash of Lea and Perrins), nosh on Kippers and Eggs à la Danny Kaye, nibble on a Dorothy Lamour salad (fresh pineapple, sliced bananas, and strawberries with cream cheese), and finish up with Strawberries Heston (strawberries with sour cream, honey, and cinnamon). For the brave or foolish, there was even a Martin and Lewis special—stewed toads and broiled birds with woodchucks on Ry-Crisp—for a mere $33.00.

Stars did engage in other activities besides eating. Despite the sweaty atmosphere, nightclubs remained popular spots to get your picture taken. The wire services employed a staff of photographers whose sole job was to stand outside the clubs' entrances and wait. Unlike today's paparazzi, the celebrity photographers of the Golden Age generally stuck to the rules: Don't come in unless you're invited, no flashbulbs during meals or performances, and no pictures of female stars holding drinks or smoking cigarettes (although sitting in front of a drink, especially if it looked clear enough to be mistaken for water, was fine).

Although not qualifying as strictly speaking "night life," shopping was another valuable tool in the search for free publicity. The stars would settle upon their favorite stores, and a mutual admiration society would form around them. According to *The Hollywood Reporter,* the most popular hairdresser to the stars was Weaver-Jackson's. For home furnishings, the in-crowd shopped at Barker Brothers. I. Magnin had the most chic outfits, Max Lichter the most beautiful flower arrangements, and Young's of Hollywood the plumpest produce and the freshest, most flavorful cheese.

Perhaps the most famous Hollywood haunt not strictly associated with dining or dancing was Schwab's Drugstore, conveniently located at 8024 Sunset Boulevard, in the crosshairs of half a dozen studio lots. Schwab's origins were humble—it was one of a chain of six stores opened by Leon, Bernard, Jack, and Martin Schwab. The Hollywood branch premiered in 1935. The legend of Lana Turner being discovered there is, by the way, false—Miss Turner, then known as Judy, was discovered by the *Reporter*'s Billy Wilkerson in the Tip Top Soda Shop, several blocks away from Schwab's. In Hollywood, of course, the truth never gets in the way of a good story, and for the next decade or so, not a day went by that you wouldn't find some ingenue perched upon one of Schwab's stools, ordering herself a tall root beer and waiting for that tap on the shoulder.

For years Schwab's fought a publicity war with the Beverly Wilshire Hotel Drugstore. The Wilshire, owned by Milton Kreis, tried to appeal to the snobs who looked down on Schwab's as a dump. Kreis sold $500 hairbrushes and installed plug-in telephones at the fountain. He published his own monthly gossip magazine, *Chatter,* and even hired his own gossip columnist, Sheilah Graham. Meanwhile, for their resident columnist, Sidney Skolsky, Schwab's built a balcony office that overlooked the entire store. Soon Schwab's was boasting that the premiere

*L*oretta Young and Rosalind Russell help sell home permanents. "Which twin has the Toni?" was the famous advertising slogan for the Toni Home Permanent company. Although not quite twins, Young and Russell obligingly curled their hair and donned matching striped dresses and twin cigarette holders to help sell the company product. The man on the right, comb in pocket, is most likely a Toni rep, keeping a close eye on the proceedings. *Photograph courtesy of Photofest, New York.*

Any movie...any party...Susan Hayward and Angela Lansbury, accompanied by their husbands, celebrate the opening night of Black Narcissus (Archer, 1947), a film with which none of them had anything to do whatsoever. Photograph courtesy of Photofest, New York.

of an obscure Italian comedy was going to be held at its counter, while the Wilshire announced a midnight shindig for the Ritz Brothers. Both parties made the columns and everybody went to bed happy.

Hollywood parties had an important role in the sociology of star-making. As anthropologist Hortense Powdermaker explains in her book *Hollywood, The Dream Factory,* "playing the social game and going to the right parties is always helpful on the road to stardom. It is important to keep literally within the range of executives' and producers' eyes. One young man, now playing featured parts, who has his eyes set on star roles, says 'I go to big parties not because I particularly enjoy them or have nothing else to do, but because it is good to be seen by the producers and directors who are there. Someone is bound to say, "Who is that handsome guy?" and then think of me for some part.'"

If one were to believe the publicity flacks, party life in the Golden Age of Hollywood was wonderful and open-ended, but most likely it was also largely mythical. Like everybody else, most actors liked to go home after a full day's work. But publicity department flacks needed to get their employees' names into the papers, and agents wanted to boost their clients' reputations. So Clark Gable was spotted wolfing down a cheeseburger at Don the Beachcomber's, Ida Lupino and Errol Flynn were caught by a photographer trying to sneak out the back door of the Cock 'N' Bull, and Loretta Young and Rosalind Russell could compete to see "which twin has the Toni" (an advertisement for Toni Home Permanent). Still, there was a certain sparkle and innocence about the game. A sense of mutual admiration, congeniality, and civility reigned.

All this began to change when the studios disappeared. Without the security blanket of the studio apparatus to protect them, stars found themselves hounded by the press and simultaneously craving their attention. The Italians invented the term "paparazzi," but Hollywood adopted it, for better and for worse. By the sixties, Hollywood night life meant blurry pictures of Elizabeth Taylor and Richard Burton and car chases. By the seventies, drug busts were as frequent as premieres. Relations between the stars and the press had become polluted by a sense of mistrust and crossed purposes. It's true that old Hollywood wasn't one big party, but there were a whole lot of nice little ones along the way. ★

Chapter 7

TOUR DE FORCE: ROAD SHOWS AND PERSONAL APPEARANCES

Mickey Rooney signs autographs—location unknown. In the early years of the war, Rooney was still a top box office draw and was in high demand at Army camps, on U.S.O. tours, and for bond drives across America. Photograph courtesy of Photofest, New York.

On an early May morning in 1942, a train pulled into Union Station in Washington, D.C., to be greeted by an adoring crowd. Within that train's luxurious confines slept one of the largest contingents of Hollywood stars ever assembled—Cary Grant, Desi Arnaz, Merle Oberon, Charles Boyer, Olivia de Havilland, Spencer Tracy, Irene Dunne, and Betty Grable, for starters. The reason for all the excitement was the arrival of the Victory Caravan, a trainload full of movie personalities crisscrossing the country to put on free shows and sell Victory Bonds to aid the Allied Forces in World War II. There was a club car open twenty-four hours a day for drinks and sandwiches, and no double-bunking—each star had his or her own private compartment.

It was not only the stars who were showing their stripes. The Victory Caravan featured new songs by Frank Loesser and Johnny Mercer. There was special material written for the performers by the famous play-writing team of George S. Kaufmann and Moss Hart, who created simple scenes demonstrating how valuable solidarity, determination, and a great sense of humor would be in the U.S. effort to win the war. By the time the train reached Washington, it had already toured the West and the South. Still to come: New York, Boston, Philadelphia, Cleveland, Detroit, Chicago, Milwaukee, Saint Louis, Saint Paul, and Des Moines.

The stars on the Victory Caravan and those who entertained enlisted men at the Hollywood Canteen and toured overseas Army and Navy bases for the USO may have been genuinely interested in helping the war effort, but they were flushed out of their private hiding places by necessity. The war had destroyed the foreign market for films, and domestic sales needed tremendous boosting. Glittering premieres with fancy cars and floodlights were disallowed. There was nothing for the stars to do but roll up their sleeves and go to work like everybody else. By the end of 1942, the stars of the Hollywood Canteen had entertained over 600,000 men and women in uniform, sold half a million packs of cigarettes, and made nearly one million chicken, tuna fish, and peanut butter and jelly sandwiches. Moviegoers around the nation found themselves alternately amused and astounded to see photographs of their favorite stars appearing in the most unlikely of poses.

The Victory Caravan was one of the more dramatic and successful examples of movie stars from different studios working together for free,

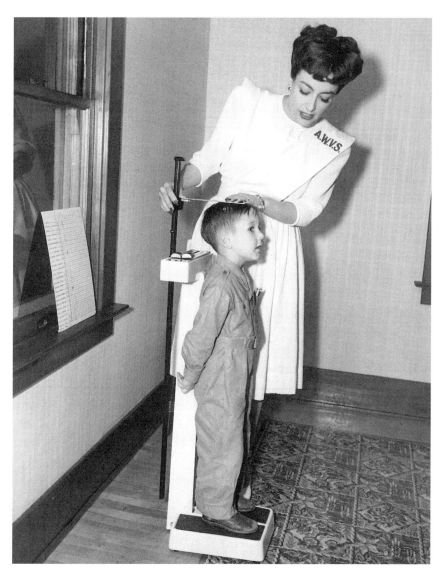

*J*oan Crawford plays nurse. Crawford donated her time and talents to the American Women's Voluntary Services, formed to help out on the home front during the Second World War. This little boy's mother, like thousands of others, was working the day shift at the Douglas Aircraft plant in Los Angeles, and the A.W.V.S. ran the nurseries needed to care for the children. For the LA branch, Miss Crawford reportedly chose the furnishings and paid the rent, as well as personally supervising the weekly height and weight checkups. *Photograph courtesy of Photofest, New York.*

for a good cause, and with nothing to promote. But it would be only partially true to mistake their altruism for selflessness. As a classic example of a "win/win" situation, the Hollywood Victory Caravan of 1942 not only raised over one billion dollars to aid the war effort (more than any other bond drive to date), it kept the names of many of Hollywood's most important stars on everyone's lips. It was good publicity. If a star wished to remain a star, he or she was contractually obliged to help promote the studio's pictures in whatever manner the studio desired. The fact that a great many of the stars found touring to be fun was beside the point.

America is a vast nation, and personal appearances and road shows have served as valuable publicity tools since the first cameras rolled. Long before Hollywood was a gleam in a producer's eye, itinerant theatrical troupes roamed the land, stopping in cities and towns of all sizes to entertain, earn a few bucks, and move on. It made sense that the nascent film industry of the earliest years of the century would instantly gravitate to the vaudevillian mode of entertainment. Early movie road shows exactly resembled stage shows, with billed acts and sideshows, often appended to already existing carnival circuits. Outside of the biggest cities, folks seeking an evening's entertainment in the years preceding the First World War would most likely attend the show in a tent, where animal tamers and arcade amusements would vie with one-reelers for their attention. The film industry grew larger and more consolidated, but it somehow never really lost its love of the old-time hoopla—parades and bands, strong men and beautiful women.

Some of the studios developed junkets for their stars that not only outdrew the Victory Caravan but rivaled the U.S. Army itself in terms of planning, deployment, and execution. Several openings are legendary. For the premiere of *Gone with the Wind* on December 15, 1939, MGM sent the entire cast to Atlanta. There were also personal appearances by Laurence Olivier (no doubt attending because he was Mr. Vivien Leigh), Carole Lombard, and Claudette Colbert (neither of whom had anything to do with the movie but were under contract to the studio). The Governor of Georgia, E.D. Rivers, proclaimed the day a state holiday. Half the population of Atlanta lined Peachtree Street to watch the motorcade that brought the stars to the Loew's Grand. The whole entourage went to New York four days later—with James Stewart, Joan Bennett, and Alice Faye.

For the premiere of *42nd Street* (1933), Warner Bros. tried to compete with Franklin Roosevelt's inauguration, putting Ruby Keeler, Dick Powell, and other stars from the film on a Superchief from LA to Washington. The studio had General Electric pay for the entire junket in return for free publicity; Powell sang "Young and Healthy" from the back of the train, and the chorus girls would trundle off at every stop and troop down to a local department store to demonstrate the latest G.E. appliances. For *Dodge City* (1939), Warner Bros. peppered the Kansas plains with several dozen marching bands, four hundred horses, a convoy of airplanes, one quarter of President Roosevelt's cabinet (Agriculture and Interior, the two departments most popular in the Farm Belt), and, last but not least, Errol Flynn.

The "smaller" junkets were not nearly so elaborate, but the stories associated with them are just as interesting and, more tellingly, the publicity probably ended up being just as good. Few care to recall the trip Frank Capra organized for himself and James Stewart to Beaumont, Texas, in March 1947, in support of *It's a Wonderful Life* (Columbia). Apparently the Jefferson Amusement Company, which ran Beaumont's largest theater, convinced the star and his director that a personal appearance would help their box office immensely. Capra had gotten nowhere with a writing contest ("Why Have You Had 'A Wonderful Life'?"), so he was game for anything. The flight to Beaumont, conducted in a tiny two-engine biplane rented at the last minute to make the final lap from Dallas, was delayed four hours due to bad weather. Despite the absence of their guests of honor, the town parade and testimonial luncheon went ahead as planned. When the star and the director finally arrived at the airport, wet and shaken, there remained only a handful of the five thousand plus who had originally shown up. The two high-school bands hired by Jefferson had long since put down their instruments and returned to their classes. Stewart and Capra made it to the screening, at least. The evening premiere went smoothly, and reportedly everyone was calm by midnight.

Darryl Zanuck's attempts at drumming up business for his presidential epic *Wilson* (Fox, 1944) were even less successful. For reasons apparent only to Zanuck, *Wilson* opened in Zanuck's hometown of Wahoo, Nebraska. The presence of Clark Gable, Tyrone Power, Joan

*L*izabeth Scott makes a personal appearance at the Carlton Theatre, Haymarket, for the London premiere of The Strange Love of Martha Ivers *(Paramount, 1946). There is a suffocating feeling to this photograph that perfectly captures a dark, and even dangerous, side to a star's exposure.*
Photograph courtesy of Photofest, New York.

Fontaine, and Gene Tierney boosted the opening-day crowds, but by the following evening, the house was virtually abandoned. One local man gave the most credible explanation. "The people of Wahoo wouldn't have come to see Woodrow Wilson if he rode down Main Street in person," he said, "so why in hell should they pay to see him in a movie?" In 1954, Zanuck sent out a self-proclaimed "ballyhoo wagon" to promote *The Egyptian* (Fox). The tour traveled 6,000 miles and included props, sets, and scenery from the film, live animals, and dozens of extras in full costume, but it didn't help. *The Egyptian* was a terrible picture, and it flopped. Nobody knows for certain how much Lizabeth Scott appreciated her London junket in support of *The Strange Love of Martha Ivers* (Paramount, 1946), but the sight of the actress crushed by the curious crowds is unnerving to behold.

Sometimes the publicity is bigger than the picture. When Howard Hawks wanted Jane Russell and Jack Beutel to make personal appearances in support of *The Outlaw* (RKO, 1943), the two stars dutifully flew up to San Francisco and carefully rehearsed a new scene Hawks had written expressly for them to perform at the premiere. With the beating of the drums and the salting of the papers, a full house awaited Russell and Beutel on the big night. The orchestra struck up a chord of anticipation. The audience began to applaud—and then the curtain got stuck, cutting off Miss Russell and Mr. Beutel from the neck up. The crowd dissolved in hysterical laughter. The "personal appearance" was cancelled. Sometimes it was more than just the stars and studios that benefited from touring. In 1950, Louisiana senator Dudley J. LeBlanc hired Mickey Rooney and Connee Boswell to lead a vaudeville show across the South. Admission to the show was one Hadacol boxtop. Hadacol was a popular cold medicine, and Senator LeBlanc owned the company.

As the studios grew more desperate and the stars began to chafe under the tight reins, tours and personal appearances grew rarer and more idiosyncratic. Some of the biggest stars loved meeting their fans, as long as the star held all the cards. Joan Crawford, with the help of her personal publicist at MGM, Milton Weiss, planned her itineraries with the precision of a presidential campaign. For one day in New York, Miss Crawford planned to be greeted by her fan club at Grand Central Station, after which there would be a shopping trip to Macy's with

Dorothy Kilgallen, an appearance at the Capitol Theater with Major Bowes and Milton Berle, concluding with sit-down interviews with every daily (and there were over a half-dozen of them), scheduled precisely ninety minutes apart.

Other stars couldn't, or wouldn't, appear in public. Bette Davis was willing to do war work but couldn't stand being ogled by fans. Eventually, disgusted with the boorish behavior of studio executives, the press, and intrusive fans alike, Katharine Hepburn wouldn't even attend her own premieres. And Judy Garland was game, but so demanding and unpredictable that the studio withheld her commitment and gambled that she'd show up for events. The day before the premiere of *A Star Is Born* (1954), Warner Bros. advanced Miss Garland $1,200 for her out-of-pocket expenses, as well as those of her personal assistant and dresser. All three persons promptly disappeared. No one was in contact with the temperamental star for over twenty-four hours. When the moment came, Garland showed, looking more glamorous than she had in years, despite being four months pregnant. She faced down the mob of fans, the live television cameras, and the incredulous stares of the studio flacks with perfect aplomb and grace. No one ever asked for her expense account report.

For every uncooperative or merely perfunctory star appearance, there would be another that would be riveting, truly heartfelt, and, most importantly, financially rewarding. Chiefly responsible for the latter category of performer were the popular radio stars of the thirties and forties. People like Bing Crosby, Frank Sinatra, Gene Autry, and Roy Rogers all had established careers as singers, radio stars, and chart-busting recording artists before they began their movie careers, and the switch to Hollywood never slowed their constant touring.

For over thirty years, until age slowed him down, Frank Sinatra toured in front of, alongside, and behind every feature film he made. "You rotate between five places," he told a national radio audience, "— the bus, the hotel room, the greasy-spoon restaurant, the dressing room, if any, and the bandstand. Then back on the bus." His personal fan club, The Swooners, wore custom-designed sweatshirts and caps emblazoned with a capital "S" and were known to engage the star himself in back-stage pickup softball games if time and circumstances allowed it.

Al Jolson at LaGuardia Airport, circa 1943. Movie stars who served in the USO were considered military personnel and were required to wear standard uniforms. This early-morning candid photograph of Jolson returning from his fourth overseas tour catches the tireless singer and actor before he had the opportunity to change into his civvies. *Photograph courtesy of Photofest, New York.*

*E*lizabeth Taylor helps make up a C.A.R.E. package. The war was over, but the studios had learned how much goodwill and free publicity their stars could earn through good deeds. MGM paid for this carefully posed photograph of Taylor tinkering with a few sprigs of fake ivy and a pair of plastic turkeys, and included in their original caption the fact that "little Miss Taylor is portraying the role of Amy in the studio's Technicolor production of Little Women." *Photograph courtesy of Photofest, New York.*

Gene Autry's "Melody Ranch" was a nationwide hit on the radio five years before his screen debut. For his film career, he hardly skipped a beat. Autry would broadcast from the top of a railroad flatcar, singing hits from his latest movie. His popularity was greatest in the South and the Southwest, and Republic Pictures sent him back out there over and over again. When Autry's star began to fade during the war, Roy Rogers' career followed a nearly identical path. The "King of the Cowboys" had been a country music star with The Sons of the Pioneers, and would think nothing of playing over 300 shows every year. The flow from popular music to film stardom has never really stopped, as evidenced by Elvis Presley and Barbra Streisand—but in their cases, the personal appearances completely ceased when their film careers took off. Elizabeth Taylor willingly posed with a wartime C.A.R.E. package as a teenager and then spent thirty-odd years away from the hustling media, only returning to the fray to raise money for AIDS charities at the end of her career.

Perhaps the world has grown too big, or the market place too huge, for a return to the so-called Golden Days of Hollywood, where you could catch Rita Hayworth at a premiere or Deanna Durbin in concert at the Hollywood Bowl. Perhaps today's movie stars are, in fact, too accessible. Movie stars still attend premieres, of course, but the stars and the events all seem the same—a limo, a wave, twenty seconds on *Entertainment Tonight.* They are seen every day on television, on videotape, at the checkout counter, and in the multiplexes. Most of them no longer have that mysterious aura that made a star appearance something special, even if in retrospect these appearances now seem simultaneously grandiose and silly. All that remains are the memories—the glimpses of the newsreels; the sound of the breathless broadcaster; those towering, tilting spotlights; and the hush of the audience before the curtain parts, the band strikes a chord, and the star comes out to say hello. ★

Agent Sidney Skolsky snags Simone Signoret's autograph. Skolsky never owned a car and depended upon his clients to shuttle him around town. *Photograph courtesy of Photofest, New York.*

Chapter 8
THE TEN-PERCENTERS:
HOLLYWOOD AGENTS

On the greased pole of Hollywood, no profession has ever occupied a more ambiguous position than that of the agent. In popular folklore, the Hollywood agent is almost equal to the Devil himself—a greedy and talentless vampire who tempts one's soul by offering profit and fame for a tithe. Of course, the truth turns out to be far less definitive—as truth often turns out to be. Hollywood agents—surprise!—are as human as the rest of us, suffering equally from frustration and ambition, feeling wildly successful one day and desperately poor the next, and treating all of humanity with equal doses of mindless cruelty and endless compassion.

Agents prowled the streets of Hollywood from the very beginning, extending the tradition of theatrical agents already in place in New York and, before that, London. Harry Reichenbach began representing clients to Metro Pictures as early as 1914. By the forties, there were over 150 registered agents in the Los Angeles area alone. As with the studios, the power among these agents was concentrated in a few large firms, most of which also owned shares of stock in the very studios with which they were negotiating.

The three kings of the agents were William Morris, Charles K. Feldman, and Myron Selznick. Morris began as a literary agent, representing the authors whose work was so desperately needed by the story-hungry studios. Like so many others in the business, he got his start working the vaudeville circuit out of New York City, but he quickly got entangled in a three-way business feud with Edward Albee (the noted playwright's father) and B.F. Keith (who started the Orpheum Theater circuit, which eventually became RKO—Radio Keith Orpheum). The end result of this feud was the concept of the independent talent agency, free from the crushing control of theater owners like Albee and Keith. Morris died in 1932, but not before starting the legendary agency which still bears his name.

Feldman began his career by offering to represent actors to the studios on the one hand, and producing films for the studios on the other—a very cozy relationship that not only increased Feldman's income dramatically but also made him extremely powerful from a business standpoint. Feldman's Achilles' heel was the fact that he stole the affection of actress Jean Howard from Louis B. Mayer, which made him Mayer's

*W*alter Connolly, Carole Lombard, and Russell Birdwell take a break for ice cream and a ciga- rette on the set of Nothing Sacred (Selznick, 1937). Birdwell was one of the most powerful agents in the history of Hollywood. He worked for the stars, for the papers, and for the studios— occasionally simultaneously—during the course of his long career. Such was the strength of his ability and reputation that no one employer ever completely trusted him, or could do without him.

Photograph courtesy of Photofest, New York.

archenemy and often put Mayer's stellar roster of stars out of his reach.

Myron Selznick was born with the enviable advantage of being producer David O. Selznick's brother. A career in the business was inevitable, but his exact route was unclear. Then, one day in 1927, young Myron, then rooming with Lewis Milestone, was asked by the shy director to speak for him at a business conference with a producer who worked for Howard Hughes. Selznick walked out of the meeting with fifteen hundred dollars a week for Milestone and a reputation for being a hard bargainer. No less an expert than Louella Parsons, a woman who understood the value of negotiating from strength, proclaimed, "Selznick made the stars aware of their power. It was he who laid the foundation for today's Hollywood, which is run by the stars and their agents."

Another prototypical Hollywood agent was Wilson Heller. Heller began his career in the teens with the miniscule General Service Studios. He worked for free in exchange for office space, and the kid at the desk next to his was Howard Hughes (funny how Hughes' name gets into everybody's business). Hughes' looks and Heller's smarts brought clients pouring in. By the twenties, Heller had signed Clara Bow, Blanche Sweet, Richard Dix, and Harold Lloyd. Unfortunately, when the Silent Era ended, Heller's power diminished, though the ambitious Hughes moved on to another quarry. With an atypical lack of bitterness, Heller gave a genial interview to *The Hollywood Reporter* long after his retirement, in which he gives us a rare view of the town as it appeared before the movie colony took complete control. Apparently, agents were needed to keep their clients out of jail as often as in the money. "Things were wilder and freer," Heller remarks. "The performers were mostly uneducated notoriety seekers. The town was wide open and the police didn't watch things so closely."

Heller is equally (and unusually) frank about the sexual activities of the stars, acknowledging as truth what everyone had suspected for years. "Among my women clients," he reports, "it was well-known around the business that only a few of them never laid a guy to get where they were—among them Bebe Daniels, Lois Wilson, and Patsy Ruth Miller. They would go to parties now and then, but they wouldn't screw …Most of the others got their jobs by laying somebody. Among the early stars, I think every damn one of them laid some guy to get ahead."

Generally, Hollywood agents preferred life away from the spotlights and the cameras—that's one of the reasons they became agents instead of actors. But inevitably, close association with the stars would thrust them into public attention, for better or (usually) for worse. In a long, three-part article that appeared in the *Saturday Evening Post* in August 1942, Alva Johnston chronicled with bemused precision the prizes and pitfalls of what he called "Hollywood's Ten Per Centers." Johnston included candid photographs of Paulette Goddard lighting Myron Selznick's cigarette and he chronicled (mostly through anonymous sources) the petty arguments, well-laid schemes, and attention-getting pranks that he believed constituted an agent's life.

In passing, the article made mention of a few of agentry's notable events, such as Selznick's brazen theft of William Powell, Kay Francis, and Ruth Chatterton from Paramount and subsequent signing with Warner Bros., as well as some of the more obscure ones, such as an error in Carole Lombard's contract which ended up requiring Selznick to pay Lombard ten percent of *his* earnings.

Many agents worked for the stars, but just as many worked for the studios—and several gleefully worked for both, often at the same time and on the same projects. The studio press agents were as genial and ruthless as their colleagues playing the field. Max Youngstein, who worked at various times for Paramount, United Artists, and dozens of independent producers planting items, brainstorming gimmicks, and looking for a piece of the action, recalled some of his notorious exploits for interviewer Chris Nelson:

> Somehow or other, my résumé came to the attention of Spyros Skouras. Skouras was an uneducated Greek who, by sheer force of personality and street smarts, became head of Fox's theater division. He wore expensive clothes but nothing matched and he could hardly speak English. So he must have been overly impressed by my two law degrees…I had special assignments that I had to do for him, which were highly confidential. I had to read the scripts, because reading English was a chore for Skouras, but he had to go into the Executive Committee meetings and talk about the pictures he was making.

So he wanted me to read them for him, and I had to deliver my reports by hand...

I tried to raise publicity to what I believed was its proper niche. Publicity was manpower. If you could create stunts, you created a feature story. You got interviews. You got unusual photographs. That, in my opinion, paid back advertising, at least. Today, publicity is a lost art, for all practical purposes. It's all licensing.

Youngstein goes on to recount his work for the opening of *Samson and Delilah* (Paramount, 1949):

I opened at the Joy Theatre, which is a second- or third-rate theater in New Orleans, and I had what we used to call a "field man"... And now I said, "Look, here's what you're making as salary. I'm going to give you two hundred and fifty dollars extra if you'll do the following stunt. I want you to get hold of two lions and I want you to put them on a leash, a chain—get 'em old and toothless but ferocious-looking—and in tandem just walk down the middle of Main Street." Two hundred and fifty bucks was a lot of money. He needed the money; he did the job. Before he got more than a block and a half, he was arrested. The picture made the front pages of all the papers in New Orleans. It was on the air on all the radio stations. The picture opened up and did more business in the first day that it had done in the previous week.

Youngstein rented retired Royal Air Force fighter jets to promote Tyrone Power in *A Yank in the RAF* (Fox, 1941) and deliberately derailed railroad cars full of circus elephants to promote a circus picture (no people or elephants were hurt during the completion of this stunt).

Paul Macnamara, who worked for many years for David O. Selznick, survived and even thrived because he was one of the few agents seemingly unaffected by his bosses' or clients' idiosyncrasies. Macnamara began as a reporter for the Hearst organization, and he never lost his sense of amusement or perspective. He began every day with the same breakfast—half a grapefruit, two soft-boiled eggs, one slice of toast, an entire pot of coffee, and copies of the *Los Angeles Times, Hollywood Reporter,* and *Variety.* While helping Selznick promote *Duel in the Sun* (1946), Macnamara ordered a four-story-tall billboard of Jennifer Jones repainted because her eyes appeared crossed when viewed from the street. He once faked a telephone call from Howard Hughes in order to keep a commercial flight from taking off. He was the first publicity agent to hire a polling firm (George Gallup), and the first to suggest saturation booking—the now-common practice of opening a picture in several dozen cities simultaneously.

Macnamara's account of Shirley Temple's wedding in 1945 is classic. In his characteristic deadpan, he writes that "the Temple wedding was planned like the invasion of Europe. Every step was planned, rehearsed, replanned, revised, and then dress-rehearsed for timing. The wedding was to take place at the Wilshire United Methodist Church on Wilshire Boulevard. Stands were erected across the street, and they were filled hours before the ceremony was to take place. We arranged to close Wilshire Boulevard for two hours in the middle of the afternoon ..." According to Macnamara, the difficulty of arranging the entire event was comparable to landing a hundred thousand troops in Europe. Howard Strickling, director of publicity at MGM, gave the wedding party the protection of the entire MGM police force. Motorcycle cops accompanied the bridal party from West Los Angeles, and there were half a dozen LA police on horseback for crowd control. Macnamara continues:

> We had a large map of the area with the route from Olympic to Wilshire and up to the side door of the church. We had timed to the minute how long it would take from the Temple house in Westwood, down Olympic, to the church on Wilshire. The bridal party was scheduled to arrive in three limos at exactly 3:55 at the side entrance, and like clockwork, they did. One of my people was at the curb with a checklist of exactly who was to be in each car. I went out to check how it was going, and right away found we were in trouble. One of the cars didn't have the right number of people. There was one person missing. It was Shirley Temple's brother. He was supposed to be in the third car. We put

in a call to the Temple house and, sure enough, he was there. He had got himself locked in the bathroom. Even with the motorcycle and the limo, it would take at least twenty-five minutes to go out and get him, but Mrs. Temple said we had to do it. And that's what we did, with the motorcycles flashing their red lights and their sirens going full blast. They made the round trip in exactly twenty-four minutes.

A good explanation for the hardened heart of the Hollywood agent, in and out of the studio's clutches, can be found in the fact that so many of them began as sportswriters, used to working on deadline and striking devil's bargains to make their stories exclusive. Arch Reeves, who worked on publicity at Paramount in the forties, was an editor at the *Los Angeles Tribune.* Harry Brandt, who ended up heading Fox's publicity department, was Reeves' assistant. Howard Strickling began as an office boy at the same paper. Dorothy Blanchard, one of the few women to enter into this men's club, started out—as so many women did—as a secretary, and wound up touring with Ava Gardner.

The lure of agency and the promise of easy money is something many people trying to break into the business—and many more already in it—found irresistible. Zeppo Marx quit his brothers' act to become an agent, a line he was certainly better suited for than comedy. Failed leading men like Jack Sherill and Gus Shy, seeing little profit in third billing, cleaned up at ten percent. Even executives occasionally took the plunge. Mike Levee quit his job as one of the top producers at Warner Bros. to try his hand at representation.

Still, it is their reputation for avarice, stupidity, and plain old buffoonery which has made Hollywood agents the fodder of so much humor. Some possibly apocryphal tales have been passed down through the generations like war stories: The agent who wrote to Thackeray care of the Modern Library, advising him that his property *Vanity Fair* might make a great movie. Or the one who wanted to sign up Goethe as a screenwriter, or the one who inquired where payment should be sent for the writer of *Hamlet.* There were agents who represented animals (Red Donohue signed up Uno, a mule) and agents who represented themselves (Ben Carter, who was black, got himself a contract by imitating one of his clients so well that the studio fired the actor and hired him to play the part). When Leland Hayward, an agent, took over Charles Brackett and Billy Wilder's contract, he ordered the veteran team to undergo a medical examination before he would sign; as counterprotection, Brackett and Wilder sent a psychiatrist to examine Hayward. The results were deemed satisfactory to all, and the deal went ahead.

The hit parade of great Hollywood press agents would have to include Jim Moran. Moran thought up many of the most notorious publicity stunts of the era. He suggested crossing a centipede with a turkey to alleviate the wartime meat shortage (think how many soldiers you could feed with two hundred turkey legs). He sat on an ostrich egg for over three weeks to help promote *The Egg and I* (Universal-International, 1947). For *The Mouse That Roared* (Columbia, 1959), Moran opened his own embassy in Washington, D.C.—the Duchy of Grand Fenwick. He rented a Mercedes, four guards in full dress uniforms, and a suite at the Shoreham Hotel, all to present himself as the ambassador from the court of an imaginary nation. Moran's specialty was the so-called "double-reverse" publicity stunt, where the duper is duped. Once he pretended to be a foreign prince who had lost some rare jewels, then hired actors to "fall" for his story. Moran told all the papers how the "actors" were fooled by his stunt, never revealing to the press that the so-called innocent victims were hired. The papers printed his version of the story, never to figure out that the entire job was a setup.

A fondly remembered roll call of the great Hollywood agents must also include Leo Guild, who once planted a four-leaf clover in a crack in the sidewalk in front of the Strand in New York for the premiere of *The Luck of the Irish* (Fox, 1948), and had it "accidentally" discovered six times each day. Guild was one of those rare breeds who would put in a lot of personal effort on behalf of his clients—he once actually lobbied the New York State Assembly to have the age of consent for marriage lowered from eighteen to seventeen in time for the opening of *Seventeen* (Paramount, 1940).

John Springer was a handsome man who parlayed his looks into nights on the town while representing Marilyn Monroe, Judy Garland, Marlene Dietrich, and Elizabeth Taylor. Meanwhile, agent Henry Willson worked the other side of the fence, specializing in beefcake and name

*J*oan Leslie and Sidney Skolsky, circa 1940. Skolsky was a funny, implike little man, which made him "safe" for scantily dressed starlets like Joan Leslie. In the world of Hollywood publicity, it was the perfect equation—he gets the power, she gets the glory, and they both get paid.
Photograph courtesy of Photofest, New York.

changes: his clients included Arthur Gelien (Tab Hunter), Francis McGowen (Rory Calhoun), and Roy Fitzgerald (Rock Hudson). The humorous side of this aggressive renaming appealed to Humphrey Bogart, who suggested to Willson he might sign on under the new name "Dungg Heap."

Not every agent in Hollywood history was a charlatan or a fool. When he wasn't on his usual job of representing his clients, Abe Lastfogel spent many hours raising money for charity. He got together with columnist Walter Winchell, studio executive Marvin Schenck, and producer Howard Dietz to hold a rally for the Navy at Madison Square Garden in 1942 that raised $142,000 in war bonds. Later Lastfogel received a Medal of Freedom for organizing the USO Camp Shows. Still, despite all this altruism, Abe Lastfogel's longest lasting contribution to Hollywood history was the chicken soup named after him on the menu at Mama Weiss' on Rodeo Drive.

Hollywood's legendary agent/imp was Sidney Skolsky. Skolsky was an extremely short and corpulent man, leading most of his clients to describe him as "pint-sized" and a few of his enemies to use the less-charitable appellation "frog." Skolsky stood apart among agents not only because of his lack of physical stature but because his office, for several decades, was in Schwab's Drugstore. Skolsky was a columnist as well as an agent. He held court at the soda counter, and when the crush grew too great for the store to reasonably conduct business, they built him a balcony office with picture windows. Skolsky once spanked Shirley Temple for accidentally sitting on his favorite hat, and once bit Louella Parsons. Although the reason for the bite has vanished, the bite itself made it into several memoirs.

Skolsky was singular amongst Hollywood agents (and amongst everyone in Hollywood, for that matter) in that he never learned to drive a car. He depended upon lifts and hitches to get him from studio to set and back to Schwab's. Is there a more perfect metaphor for the sado-masochistic relationship between agent and star than the image of Skolsky, the four-foot-plus butterball, thumb out in the breeze, hoping that some starlet in a silver roadster will weigh the hidden benefits of his company against the notable deficits, and give him a ride? ★

Chapter 9
GRAPHIC LANGUAGE: ADVERTISING AND THE MOVIES

*T*he Screen Services Art Department at work, 1935. Since all that remains of old Hollywood are the movies themselves (and a few tourist-oriented recreations), it is easy to forget what a company town Los Angeles was. The web of entanglements was impenetrable—wig-weavers, button-sewers, electricians, sound engineers, set painters, caterers, nurses, tutors...all connected to the business, one way or another.

Photograph courtesy of Photofest, New York.

The ultimate goal of every motion picture studio executive, every technician, and every actor was to get as many people as possible to see their pictures. Without box office success, prestige, fame, and artistic merit would vanish like a haze. Publicity was the lifeblood of the business, but it arrived in many guises. Personal appearances, marketing tie-ins, contests, fashion plates, and old-fashioned hoopla all played key roles in the process of selling films and their stars, but no public-relations tool was as pervasive or effective as good old-fashioned advertising. Americans saw advertisements in their daily newspapers, on posters and billboards, or heard it in their local theater or on the radio. Ads were literally unavoidable.

Hollywood's emphasis on advertising was a direct result of the increasing importance of advertising to American business. In the era of laissez-faire capitalism that created the economic boom of the late nineteenth century, business counted on the public's ignorance to generate profit. The biggest corporations controlled how products were made, how they were marketed, and how much they would cost. All this came to an end after the First World War, when a new generation of well-educated, middle-class consumers began to gain some control over the economic circumstances of their existence. Products multiplied, markets fragmented, and people demanded both information and responsibility from their purveyors. In a panic, industry turned to public-relations managers to lubricate the previously rusty channels of communication between businesses and consumers.

By the twenties, large advertising agencies such as J. Walter Thompson, Blackett, Sample & Hummert, and Lord & Thomas were developing the basis for modern market research and publishing how-to books that explained their discoveries. These books were manna to the motion picture studio publicity departments, who were eager to exploit their product in the most complete and up-to-date manner possible. The studios learned many lessons at the feet of their agency predecessors, such as the value of polling, the need to simplify the message, how personalities can drive profits, and—most of all—the power of advertising. By the mid-thirties, sponsorship had become the catchword of the nation. Public figures were willing to take advantage of their new, media-driven recognition, and the advertising agencies were more than eager to reward them. Blackett, Sample & Hummert spent over four million dollars in 1934 to purchase radio advertising for Bayer Aspirin, Ovaltine, and College Inn Soups, amongst others, while their principal rival, J. Walter Thompson, signed up Chase & Sanborn Coffee, Fleischmann's Margarine, Carter's Ink, Eastman Kodak, and Kraft Foods.

Motion picture advertising came in several different forms and from several different directions. From the studios, the distributors and exhibitors would receive color and black-and-white posters and trailers. The newspapers were sent ready-to-publish ads, with the name and address of the theater and the time of the shows to be filled in by the paper. Radio stations used either prerecorded speeches or read "suggested" one-minute scripts. Meanwhile, theater managers could advertise on their own, and could make extra money by accepting on-screen commercials and industrial shorts from automobile makers, oil and tobacco companies, and—especially in rural America—farm equipment manufacturers and seed providers. Cheapest of all was street-hawking, an ageless technique heavily dependent upon the willingness of the local boys and girls to make themselves appear ridiculous in front of their peers.

This cacophony of endorsements was enhanced by subliminal forms of advertising, the kind which today would be called "product endorsements." The airwaves were filled with the sound of movies being peddled—Rudy Vallee would sing the latest theme songs or Kay Kyser would play them on the Kraft Music Hall. Entire scenes from new releases could be heard on Calvacade of America and Lux Radio Theater—the latter also selling lots of Lux soap. Walter Winchell and Dorothy Kilgallen would mention their favorite films and stars in their daily radio shows and newspaper columns. All the popular magazines of the day were packed with colorful, full-page advertisements for cigarettes, appliances, apparel, beauty products, and home furnishings dutifully endorsed by stars.

Poster campaigns were bigger and catchier, but in reality they probably didn't raise the profit margin nearly as dramatically as a good word from Kate Smith. Quite often the movie scene advertised on the poster was nowhere to be found in the finished picture. Even the stars themselves were fundamentally cutouts: a common practice was to pose a

*T*hree willing cowgirls shill for I Shot Jesse James *(Lippert/Screen Guild, 1948). The shirts don't match, which suggests that the theater manager got off cheap.* Photograph courtesy of Photofest, New York.

body double for the long, boring poster shoot and then superimpose the star's face on the finished layout. The posters were beautifully designed, however, and the best of them qualify as works of art in themselves, however oblique their connection to the movie they were selling.

After posters, the most visible motion picture advertisements were trailers. "Coming Attractions" have become a permanent and extremely valuable piece of the promotional puzzle, as the studios quite rightly perceived that nothing can sell a picture better than the picture itself, even in an idealized, three-minute fragment. When the first trailers were produced in the twenties, the studios had nothing to do with them—they were made by independent film companies. Eventually, one of these companies, the National Screen Service Corporation, arranged an exclusive contract with the Big Five to create all their trailers. The studios would ship unused or duplicate footage to the NSSC, where it would be edited and shipped back to Los Angeles for approval. Once approved, the footage was quickly duplicated and shipped to the big regional exchanges in New York and Chicago, where it was duplicated again and mailed to the district sales offices. Eventually, this complicated process grew too costly and inefficient to sustain, and the studios began to make their own trailers—a practice that to this day continues to sell movies.

Hollywood was hard-pressed to come up with print campaigns that made as splashy an impression as the trailers, but this was not for lack of trying. For *Trader Horn* (MGM, 1931), the studio tried a billboard campaign in Hawaiian (the picture was set in the South Pacific), but this ending up amusing the public more than intriguing them. For *Objective: Burma* (Warner Bros., 1945), the print ads pushed Hollywood's first acting snake, a twenty-five-foot python (they neglected to mention how well he spoke his lines). The brains behind the studio advertising campaigns could never be accused of overestimating the intelligence of their audience. Producer Alexander Korda was so afraid that people would fail to recognize the hero of his film *Rembrandt* (London Films, 1936) that he offered free passes to anyone who could prove they owned one of the master's paintings. And, of course, there's always Jane Russell—to whom all mediums were exploitable—on the billboard for *The Outlaw* (Howard Hughes, 1943), her breasts protruding to the limit that gravity and the safety of passersby below them would allow.

These sorts of excesses were the inevitable result of years of unsuccessful attempts at self-regulation by the publicity industry. Just as the Motion Picture Production Code set a standard for moral behavior which proved irresistible to violate, so too did the International Motion Picture Advertising Association, which came up with its own code, implemented early in the thirties. Its tenets were just as high-minded and unenforceable as the Production Code. The whole of it is worth quoting, if only to gain a taste of the subtle hypocrisy that raged throughout the industry at the time:

The provisions of the code shall apply to press books, annual announcements of product, trade and newspaper advertisements, trailers, outdoor displays, novelties, and all other forms of motion picture exploitation.

1. We subscribe to the Code of Business Ethics of the International Advertising Association, based on truth and integrity.

2. Good taste shall be the guiding rule of motion picture advertising.

3. Illustrations and text in advertising shall faithfully represent the pictures themselves.

4. No false or misleading statements shall be used directly or implied by type of arrangements or by distorted quotations.

5. No text illustration shall ridicule or tend to ridicule any religion or religious faith; no illustration of character in clerical garb shall be shown in any but a respectful manner.

6. The historical institutions and nationals of all countries shall be represented with fairness.

7. Profanity and vulgarity shall be avoided.

8. Pictorial and copy treatment of officers of the law shall not be of such a nature as to undermine their authority.

9. Specific details of crime inciting imitation shall not be used.

10. The motion picture advertisers shall bear in mind the provision of the production code that the use of liquor in American life shall be restricted to the necessities of characterization and plot.

*I*n the early days of Hollywood, staged events were a common way to help the new business become known and accepted by the neighborhood. Here, a local couple chooses to tie the knot under the benevolent marquee of the 1925 MGM comedy **Cheaper to Marry**. *Photograph courtesy of Photofest, New York.*

11. Nudity, with meretricious purpose and salacious postures, shall not be used.

12. Court actions relating to censorship of pictures or other censorship disputes are not to be capitalized in advertising.

How effectively this code was enforced was an open question. To the Jews, Blacks, and Asians who were largely invisible in the advertisements, as they were on the screen, it meant very little. One's definition of "good taste" obviously needs to be wide if it is to allow for Jane Russell. An elaborate system of appeals, in which an offending producer could take his case first to appointed members of the International Motion Picture Advertising Association and then to their Board of Directors, guaranteed that any advertisement would have saturated the market long before a ban could be imposed. In the end, the Advertiser's Code, like the Production Code, merely served as a bargaining point, and the studios were quite willing to bargain away everything in exchange for a tidy profit.

By the end of the fifties, the motion picture industry was heavily dependent upon their archrival, television, for advertising revenue. MGM provided its exhibitors with a sheet of detailed instructions on how to handle the upstart invader, proving its intention to dominate TV advertising with the same sledgehammer it used to dominate radio:

MGM leads the big parade in TV spot announcement campaigns by working out highly selective schedules geared to reach specific audiences... MGM television commercials are sound-on-film, produced to allow time for a station announcer to include local theatre names and playdates on each spot telecast... There's music... there's laughter... there's drama packed into MGM's TV film commercials and radio announcements. MGM stars themselves, top announcers, actors, and commentators contribute to making these sales-aids the finest motion picture spots on the air.

TV appearances: Guest appearances of MGM stars in connection with new policy of TV Saturation Campaign. Arrangements made with Ed Sullivan to advertise seven or eight important MGM pictures on his highly rated national network show, *The Ed Sullivan Show,* and many other network programs.

As might be expected, *Gone with the Wind* (MGM, 1939) deserves the prize for Most Concerted Advertising Campaign in Film History, as much for its creativity as for its success. MGM publicity director Howard Strickling pulled out all the stops for the studio's biggest premiere. The press book was printed on heavy-coated colored stock and ran over fifty pages. It included for rental the fifty-foot cutout of Clark Gable and Vivien Leigh that adorned the marquee of the Fox Theatre in Atlanta where the picture debuted. The New York premiere was held in two theaters—the Astor and the Capitol—and was broadcast live on television, the first film ever to do so.

The studio was not content to blanket the nation with giant cutouts of the stars, full-page newspaper advertisements, embossed copies of Margaret Mitchell's novel, radio spots featuring the stars, and a magazine campaign which converted untold sheaves of the nation's general-interest pages more or less into promo fodder. It also exploited *Gone with the Wind* with unprecedented (and unsurpassed) tie-ins. One could purchase matching Rhett and Scarlett cast-iron bookends, Scarlett chocolates (Prissy peppermints, Rhett caramels, and Melanie molasses), Madame Alexander Scarlett O'Hara dolls (in continuous production since 1939), a cookbook (free with each purchase of a tube of Pebeco toothpaste), as well as copies of costume designer Walter Plunkett's hair nets, brassieres, corsets, dress patterns, hats, veils, scarves, jewels, and wrist-watches.

These incidentals helped with the initial hoopla, but it is the four-color poster which has come to represent *Gone with the Wind* for all generations. This classic image of the larger-than-life Clark Gable embracing an equally monumental Vivien Leigh above a vividly burning city of Atlanta is the quintessential publicity icon of the Golden Age of Hollywood. It has frozen for all time a moment of action and adventure, when Hollywood—and Hollywood publicity—was King. ★

A couple of coeds and anonymous gentlemen help promote *The Egg and I* (1949). A poor studio (Universal-International) and a down-home story line (introducing Ma & Pa Kettle) make for an old-fashioned bit of hoopla on the well-manicured lawn of some unidentified suburb. *Photograph courtesy of Photofest, New York.*

Chapter 10

BANK ON IT: MOVIE PROMOTION GIMMICKS

AND

No gimmicks were needed to attract crowds to silent movies—movies *were* the gimmick. No one had ever seen moving pictures before, and the sheer novelty of it all caused quite a sensation. If any advertising was called for, campaigns were quickly adopted to fit the prevailing media of the day—signboards, newspaper advertisements, and posters. Carnival attractions called for carnival hoopla.

With the proliferation of electricity and the advent of sound, motion picture advertising advanced in scale and scope. On the marquee outside the theater, a movie's title and the names of its stars could be brilliantly illuminated by electric light. Inside, enormous cutout figures of the stars greeted customers in the lobby. The largest theaters hired their own sign-painters and sound trucks. This sufficed in the Roaring Twenties, when new theaters opened weekly and everyone could afford the price of a picture. But when the Depression hit America in 1929, the movie business was not exempt from hardship. Studio revenues dropped, payrolls were slashed, and production slowed down. Desperate moviemakers scrambled to discover new ways to increase patronage. Suddenly, conventional methods of appealing to people's intelligence were abandoned for campaigns dependent on greed, vanity, and voyeurism. This strategy worked, and the business has never once looked back.

The huge number and variety of promotional gimmicks available to motion picture exhibitors in the thirties were not entirely the result of independent thinking on the part of shrewd and cynical theater managers. The studios wanted to control the advertising and keep a close watch on every aspect of a picture's promotional campaign. Most of the studios, MGM included, offered their exhibitors a number of options, usually beyond the means of an everyday promoter. For instance, the studio could arrange for personal appearances by the movie's stars. It could deliver the original costumes. It could provide the exhibitor with trailers, posters, and sound recordings. It could even guarantee a full program of quality films year round.

Press books, as noted earlier, were important promotional tools. But their value to the pictures usually went far beyond their informational content—the usual collection of overblown statistics, phony interviews, and cheat sheets. In virtually every press book, exhibitors were given

A handkerchief promoting MGM's Little Women *(1949). Every now and then, a promotional gimmick actually turned out to be not only useful but beautiful. The original object, issued in sensual rayon and in a rainbow of evanescent colors, would undoubtedly flatter any woman's features.*

Photograph courtesy of the Helen Louise Allen Textile Collection, Madison, Wisconsin.

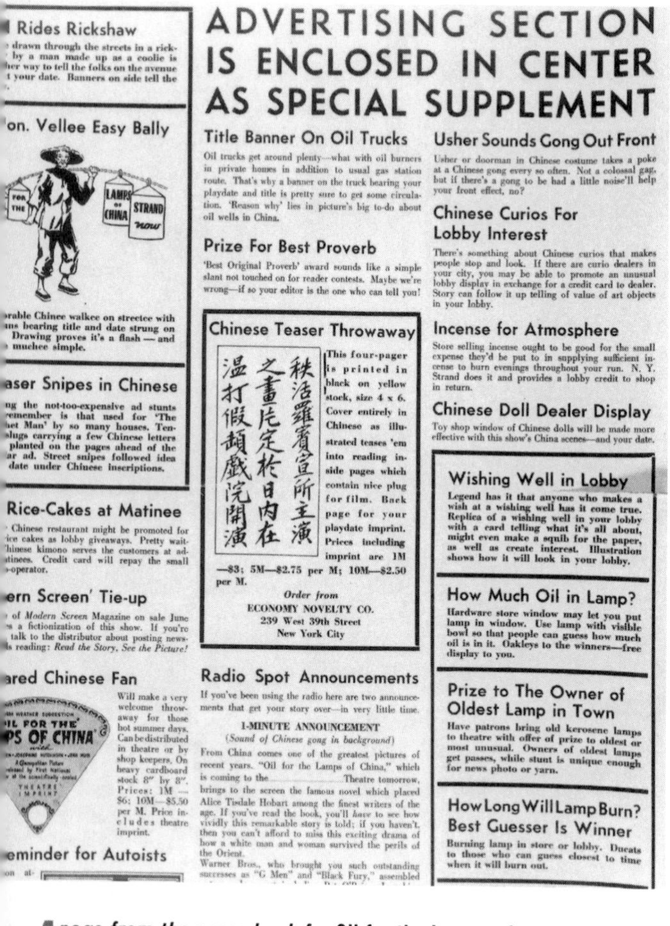

Left column fragments (partial text from edge)

Rides Rickshaw

...drawn through the streets in a rick-...by a man made up as a coolie is ...her way to tell the folks on the avenue ...f your date. Banners on side tell the

...on. Vellee Easy Bally

...orable Chince walkee on streetee with ...me bearing title and date strung on ...Drawing proves it's a flash — and ...a muchee simple.

...aser Snipes in Chinese

...ng the not-too-expensive ad stunts ...remember is that used for "The ...het Man" by so many houses. Ten-...shup carrying a few Chinese letters ...planted on the pages ahead of the ...ar ad. Street snipes followed idea ...date under Chinese inscriptions.

...Rice-Cakes at Matinee

...Chinese restaurant might be promoted for ...ice cakes as lobby giveaways. Pretty wait-...hinese kimono serves the customers at ad-...atinees. Credit card will repay the small ...-operator.

...ern Screen' Tie-up

...of Modern Screen Magazine on sale June ...s a fictionization of this show. If you're ...talk to the distributor about posting news-...h reading: Read the Story, See the Picture!

...ared Chinese Fan

Will make a very welcome throw-away for those hot summer days. Can be distributed in theatre or by shop keepers. On heavy cardboard stock 8" by 8". Prices: 1M — $6; 10M—$5.50 per M. Price includes theatre imprint.

...eminder for Autoists

ADVERTISING SECTION IS ENCLOSED IN CENTER AS SPECIAL SUPPLEMENT

Title Banner On Oil Trucks

Oil trucks get around plenty—what with oil burners in private homes in addition to usual gas station route. That's why a banner on the truck bearing your playdate and title is pretty sure to get some circulation. 'Reason why' lies in picture's big to-do about oil wells in China.

Prize For Best Proverb

'Best Original Proverb' award sounds like a simple slant not touched on for reader contests. Maybe we're wrong—if so your editor is the one who can tell you!

Chinese Teaser Throwaway

秋活羅賣宣所主演
之畫庄定於日内在
温打假頭戲院開演

—$3; 5M—$2.75 per M; 10M—$2.50 per M.

This four-pager is printed in black on yellow stock, size 4 x 6. Cover entirely in Chinese as illustrated teases 'em into reading inside pages which contain nice plug for film. Back page for your playdate imprint. Prices including imprint are 1M

Order from
ECONOMY NOVELTY CO.
239 West 39th Street
New York City

Radio Spot Announcements

If you've been using the radio here are two announcements that get your story over—in very little time.

1-MINUTE ANNOUNCEMENT

(Sound of Chinese gong in background)

From China comes one of the greatest pictures of recent years. "Oil for the Lamps of China," which is coming to the _____ Theatre tomorrow, brings to the screen the famous novel which placed Alice Tisdale Hobart among the finest writers of the age. If you've read the book, you'll have to see how vividly this remarkable story is told; if you haven't, then you can't afford to miss this exciting drama of how a white man and woman survived the perils of the Orient. Warner Bros., who brought you such outstanding successes as "G Men" and "Black Fury," assembled

Usher Sounds Gong Out Front

Usher or doorman in Chinese costume takes a poke at a Chinese gong every so often. Not a colossal gag, but if there's a gong to be had a little noise'll help your front effect, no?

Chinese Curios For Lobby Interest

There's something about Chinese curios that makes people stop and look. If there are curio dealers in your city, you may be able to promote an unusual lobby display in exchange for a credit card to dealer. Story can follow it up telling of value of art objects in your lobby.

Incense for Atmosphere

Store selling incense ought to be good for the small expense they'd be put to in supplying sufficient incense to burn evenings throughout your run. N. Y. Strand does it and provides a lobby credit to shop in return.

Chinese Doll Dealer Display

Toy shop window of Chinese dolls will be made more effective with this show's China scenes—and your date.

Wishing Well in Lobby

Legend has it that anyone who makes a wish at a wishing well has it come true. Replica of a wishing well in your lobby with a card telling what it's all about, might even make a squib for the paper, as well as create interest. Illustration shows how it will look in your lobby.

How Much Oil in Lamp?

Hardware store window may let you put lamp in window. Use lamp with visible bowl so that people can guess how much oil is in it. Oakleys to the winners—free display to you.

Prize to The Owner of Oldest Lamp in Town

Have patrons bring old kerosene lamps to theatre with offer of prize to oldest or most unusual. Owners of oldest lamps get passes, while stunt is unique enough for news photo or yarn.

How Long Will Lamp Burn? Best Guesser Is Winner

Burning lamp in store or lobby. Ducats to those who can guess closest to time when it will burn out.

Right page

WHICH TYPE MAKE-UP FO

Here's What the Stars of "Dark Victor

BETTE DAVIS   **GERALDINE**

Mat 107—15c

MEDIUM SKIN with BLONDE HAIR

With medium skin and light-blonde hair, Bette Davis is an outstanding example of this type beauty. Below are her make-up suggestions:

POWDER — Peach
ROUGE — Blush
MASCARA — Brown
LIPSTICK — Blush
EYE SHADOW — Purple

FAIR SKIN wi

Geraldine Fitz... dark hair and ... fect example ... type. Here are ... suggestions:

POWDER — ...
ROUGE — ...
MASCARA — ...
LIPSTICK — ...
EYE SHADO...

(Publicity Story)   (Publi

'Hint of Rouge Sufficient' Bette Davis Tells Blondes

"A clear, lovely skin is the blonde's most precious beauty asset," states Bette Davis, the exquisite blonde star of "Dark Victory", which will open at

Brunettes Nee... Says Ne...

"Warmth of color ... beauty asset," is the opi... lovely Irish star who ma...

Captions

A page from the press book for Oil for the Lamps of China (Warner Bros., 1935). The movie is much better than this largely racist collection of gimmicks would lead you to believe. *Photograph courtesy of the Wisconsin Center for Film and Theater Research, Madison, Wisconsin.*

A page from the press book for Dark Victory (Warner Bros., 1939). Popular "women's pictures" were opportunities for the fashion and cosmetics industri... to capitalize on a star's appeal. *Photograph courtesy of the Wisconsin Center for Film and Theater Research, Madison, Wisconsin.*

concrete (if often lunatic) ideas for promotional gimmicks guaranteed to bring some kind of attention to their feature. The publicity departments of all of the major studios (and most of the minor ones) built press books for every new release. All of them were chock-full of promotional gimmicks. The importance of the film mattered little—no opportunity for increased revenue was allowed to slide.

In the press book for *The Old Maid* (1939), starring Bette Davis and Miriam Hopkins, Warner Bros. included several pages of fashion and makeup tips, guidelines on how to organize "women's discussion groups" in the community, instructions on how to learn a new dance called "The Old Maid" (as demonstrated in the movie), as well as the usual book tie-ins and magazine subscription offers. For the gangster picture *Numbered Men* (Warner Bros., 1930), the press book included illustrations of a model wearing Jantzen bathing suits, a Helbros wristwatch, La France rings, and evening frocks, all modeled after those worn by Bernice Claire in the picture. These illustrations included the address and telephone number of the companies that sold the merchandise, the better to alert local haberdashers to stock up in advance of the show. For *Oil for the Lamps of China* (Warner Bros., 1935), the studio resorted to racist language and fortune-cookie novelties to gain attention.

Throughout the thirties and forties, studio press books grew bolder and fatter, and the gimmicks grew even wilder. Promotion for *Red River* (United Artists, 1948) included advertisements for Winchester rifles and small arms (as featured in the picture), with ready-to-order counter displays for your local gun shop. The studio encouraged its exhibitors to coordinate the release of *Red River* in their town with a rifle tournament sponsored by the local gun club, ROTC, or police. In addition, musicals would get a boost from recordings from the score. Five songs from the Warner Bros. musical remake of *One Sunday Afternoon* (1948) were recorded by Jo Stafford, Jane Pickens, and Buddy Clark and the Modernaires, all popular singing stars of the day. The sheet music and records were available for sale in the lobby. The press book for *On Your Toes* (Warner Bros., 1939) featured a tie-in with Capezio footwear, House of Westmore makeup, and Kneelast stockings.

Campaigns of this sort were usually hit-or-miss affairs; the studio hoped it would make up from susceptible customers what it lost in over-

Star

strongest
tzgerald,
m debut

head. For the so-called prestige pictures, for which the studio expected a much greater financial return, the press books (and subsequent gimmicks) were more elaborate. *Now, Voyager* (1942) is perhaps the classic example. Warner Bros. held a contest to see how many fans could guess the names of movie titles based upon other famous quotations. There was a book tie-in ("from the best-selling novel that shocked Boston speechless!"). There were life-size cutouts of Bette Davis, Paul Henreid, and Claude Rains available for the lobby. Warner's Bros.' publicity department designed nearly three dozen different posters, in several sizes. Exhibitors were even offered a choice of tag lines for banners, ranging from the mild to the provocative: "For a woman, there's always an excuse…," "Don't pity me…in our few moments together, I found a joy that most women can only dream of!" "She didn't know where she was drifting—and she didn't care!" For *Dark Victory* (1939), Warner Bros. invented copy-ready makeup tips from stars Bette Davis and Geraldine Fitzgerald, to insert into women's magazines and the homemaker sections of daily newspapers.

When producer Mervyn LeRoy remade *Little Women* (MGM, 1949), he worked with Les Paterson, director of radio for MGM Radio Attractions, to produce a tie-in with Hallmark Cards and Storybook Dolls. Storybook produced miniature replicas of all the "Little Women"— Margaret O'Brien, Janet Leigh, June Allyson, and Elizabeth Taylor. When the movie was released, the dolls were shipped to stores across America and the stars were booked on the Hallmark radio show. The studio also underwrote an attractive handkerchief imprinted with scenes from the picture and portraits of the stars, available in finer stores eveywhere.

With press books, there was never any pretense that the exhibitor was anything other than a middleman. The books would come with the names and addresses of businesses across the nation who would be willing to provide novelty perfumes, dresses, cigarette cases, wigs, cigars, guns, games, toys—you name it—to help with a specific picture's promotion. Price sheets for lobby cards, posters, head shots, and scenes in black-and-white and color (even if the movie itself was only in black-and-white) would be included with every kit.

The industry paid special attention to its female fans. While the men still earned the bulk of the money, the women spent it—at least on so-

*J*oan Crawford poses in front of a life-size Irene costume sketch. Crawford was willing to do any-thing to help her career, her pictures, and her image. If this meant spending long hours in front of the makeup mirror and still cameras or getting stuck with pins during a fitting and smiling gallantly throughout the entire ordeal, she would do it. *Photograph courtesy of Photofest, New York.*

A display window advertising Daphne Du Maurier's novel Rebecca. When David O. Selznick made the picture in 1940, the novel had been a bestseller for nearly a year. In this case, the picture capitalized on the book, just as Gone with the Wind did (Selznick again). Note how the book jacket incarnates the first Mrs. De Winter, something the movie never did. And what, exactly, is the appeal of facsimile autographs of the author and stars? *Photograph courtesy of Photofest, New York.*

called luxury items. Nearly every kit contained sheets of makeup and hairdressing tips, complete with products for sale. All the clothes worn by the female stars were available off the rack in the neighborhood department stores—this tie-in was courtesy of Bernard Waldman and the Modern Merchandising Bureau. Waldman would receive copies of the dress patterns in advance of filming, and his staff would trace, sew, and ship the dresses in time for the opening. Waldman started Modern Merchandising in 1930, and by the end of the decade, he had half a dozen custom labels producing copies of the stars' costumes. In connection with *The Buccaneer* (Paramount, 1938), one could purchase blouses called "The Boss," "The General," and "Dominique," each one sewn with the label "A Buccaneer Fashion, inspired by *The Buccaneer, a Paramount Picture.*" Waldman required that his line be restricted to only one store in each city. Such exclusivity only increased the public demand for his fashions.

When a major motion picture was based upon a best-selling novel, the studios would also lose no time coordinating an elaborate illustrated edition of the original text, usually with the full cooperation of the delighted (and enriched) author and or publisher. Occasionally a studio would go beyond the book, as evidenced by the eternally shrewd MGM, which managed to extend the reach of *Gone with the Wind* (1939) all the way into window treatments and to position *Ben Hur* (1959) directly over the customer's heart with a chariot logo on a golf shirt.

Despite these intensely coordinated efforts, the studio-inspired hoopla was sometimes still not enough. As Depression-era dollars dwindled away, exhibitors kept dreaming up new ways to entice customers into the theater. Most of these ideas had nothing to do with the picture being exhibited, and in fact, the studios continually battled with overly independent-minded exhibitors who either refused to share their windfalls with the parent company or behaved in a manner too close to extralegal for the companies to tolerate.

Some of the gimmicks dreamed up by the independents proved quite practical in the midst of the nation's grave economic crisis. Bank Nights, marketed and eventually copyrighted by Charles U. Yeager, a Twentieth Century-Fox West Coast theater manager, were basically lotteries. A patron entering the theater could write his or her name next to a number in a ledger book kept in the lobby, and the theater would keep a drum full of corresponding numbers on the side of the stage. At the end of the day, a number would be drawn and one lucky patron would win fifty or a hundred dollars. The theater's take of the extra admissions would more than equal the prize money. Sometimes enterprising managers would go one better than Bank Night by coaxing goods from local businesses in exchange for free advertising, and then give the gifts away to patrons. In this manner, people could go to the movies and come home with sets of dinner plates, makeup kits, bicycles, and sometimes even automobiles.

Still, box office receipts continued to plunge to an all-time low by 1936. Desperation set in. Children were admitted for the price of a bottle-cap. (The house would earn a profit on the candy the kids would buy.) There were quiz shows and spelling bees. Dogs, cats, and even Shetland ponies were given away, hopefully to responsible households. There were star look-alike contests, and all sorts of amateur acts—talent shows, magicians, dancers, and singers. There were gin rummy tournaments, dance marathons, and "slave" auctions. Most of these contests involved some form of talent, since Bank Night–type promotions were almost immediately declared to be a form of illegal gambling. Even double features were imperiled for a while because the studios, bless their altruistic little hearts, claimed that the practice restricted free trade.

The roots of showmanship in street-level movie promotion ran deep. "Exploitation" was not a dirty word. Most of the men who ran theaters were raised in the culture of the "can-do" philosophy that permeated all aspects of American society as it boomed and prospered in the first two decades of the century. Selling was a religion, and these men even had their bible, *Charles "Chick" Lewis Presents The Encyclopedia of Exploitation,* by Bill Hendricks and Howard Waugh. Published in 1937, *The Encyclopedia of Exploitation* is literally a listing of 1,001 ideas, beginning with No. 1, "Telling the World," and ending with No. 1001, "Check and Double-Check." Along the way, there are suggestions on how to pull off beauty pageants, hire a parachutist, print buttons, run phony screen tests, hire cigarette girls, rent circus animals, tie in department stores, cook breakfasts, outfit marching bands, and design your own lobby displays. There are ninety entries alone under the heading "radio,"

GONE WITH THE WIND

Window glamour from the "Old South" translated into smart, modern treatments for homes of today...by Kirsch

*S*ample layout for a home design advertisement. The appeal of Gone with the Wind *(both the Selznick movie, 1939, and Margaret Mitchell's novel, 1936) was so strong that even the most casual of references was gold for selling. This ornate but thoroughly modern sitting room bears no resemblance to either the real Old South or William Cameron Menzies' set designs for the film.*
Photograph courtesy of Photofest, New York.

A golf shirt to commemorate MGM's release of Ben Hur (1959). It's just a short walk from the tee to the amphitheater for any well-dressed man. Note the chariot-wheel buttons.

Photograph courtesy of Photofest, New York.

150 under the heading "Street Bally," and nearly two hundred under "Window Displays." An ambitious theater manager need only to try out one idea per week and he'd have enough exploitation to keep his palace freshly stocked with gimmicks for years.

Hendricks and Waugh's advice is always clear and direct, if not very practical. "A local ambulance company might station an ambulance in front of the theater," they advise. "It can be bannered to call attention to the fact that it is stationed there for the benefit of those unable to withstand the thrills." One hopes that no one in the town needed the services of that ambulance, or took the advice under the heading "Dope": "Capsules, obtained in quantity from a wholesale druggist, are filled with an imprinted, wound-up slip of paper ... it reads 'Dope on _____ (attraction).'" Who, exactly, was going to fill those capsules with tiny pieces of paper? Not to mention the message delivered by handing out free, unlabeled narcotics to children.

The Encyclopedia of Exploitation represents a perfect microcosm of the style, language, and habits of American showmen of the age. First, "Chick" Lewis introduces the authors in the breezy, all-business language of the day, claiming that "every conceivable phase of show-selling has been tabulated and condensed so that the busy men who run theatres and sell the shows can find what they are looking for with a minimum of effort and with a maximum of results. No words or ideas are wasted. Before they could find their way into this volume, they had to pass the acid test of practicability and actual use. Wherever the element of doubt existed as to the chances for the success of any idea, it was deliberately left out."

Hendricks and Waugh's tabulations provide social snapshots of the world of the little movie house on Main Street. For idea No. 52, "Girl and Cutout Letters," the pair suggested recruiting attractive young women to roam about town spelling out the name of the movie in five-foot-high letters. No. 485 involved canaries—the poor birds would have the letters which spelled out the name of the picture roped around their necks, and prizes were offered to moviegoers who could catch the birds randomly, getting the letters in the correct order. No. 841, simply called "Beard" asked promoters to get their local tonsorial parlor into the act as judges for a beard-growing contest. And there were 998 more.

Another oblique way to sell tickets was to produce trinkets imprint-ed with movie stars' images in series and then convince a buyer (usual-ly a young woman or an older child) that their "collection" was incom-plete if they didn't have every piece. In this manner, ordinary people with very limited incomes could be made to feel as up-to-date as any denizen of the Park Avenue auction houses.

The idea of "collectibles" was built into the Hollywood hoopla mill from the onset. Long before motion pictures were a gleam in Louis B. Mayer's eye, tobacco companies were marketing cigarette trading cards to young men. Naturally the tobacco companies moved in to exploit the popularity of movie stars as quickly as possible. Cards featuring the faces of the famous stars of the day were issued by the Hill, Job, and Players Companies in sets of fifty and inserted into packs of cigarettes from the early teens to the mid-fifties. The Hood Ice Cream Company (and later Dixie Cups) printed stars' photographs on their novelty ice-cream lids and encouraged young collectors to keep eating ice cream until their sets were complete.

Independent-minded exhibitors were an inexhaustible font of inspi-ration for exploitation gimmicks. One theater in Texas hired a girl and dressed her up as a Pony Express rider to carry a copy of the print of *Wells Fargo* (Paramount, 1937) 250 miles from the nearest exchange. In New York, a theater showing Jeanette MacDonald and Nelson Eddy in *Sweethearts* (MGM, 1938) offered any couple who asked for it a free taxi ride to the city's Marriage Bureau after the show. (Twelve couples took them up on the offer). A theater in Minneapolis offered $25 to any girl who would attend their screening of *One Hundred Men and a Girl* (Universal, 1937) with one hundred escorts.

By the end of the forties, the "Age of Innocence" for movie gimmicks was coming to an end, and the "Age of Experience" was about to begin. Americans had grown used to the soft sell of posters, giveaways, and trailers, but new competition from television had drastically cut into Hollywood's audience. A new breed of showmen arrived on the scene, independent of the old Hollywood studio system and not beholden to it. Exploitation began to acquire the air of immorality and permissiveness that it has kept to this day.

Sex was always a surefire way to sell a picture. The makers of the

A state-of-the-art marquee, circa 1953. As television sets began invading America's homes, movie-goers demanded to be treated like stars themselves. Creature comforts like air-conditioning and gimmicks like 3-D helped pump up box office sales for a while, but the era was slowly coming to an end. Photograph courtesy of The Museum of the City of New York, New York, Benn Mitchell Collection.

obscure independent film *Mom and Dad* (Hallmark/Hygienic, 1948) advertised that their picture included footage of a baby actually being born, and distributed "marriage manuals" during the intermission. There was no end to pictures featuring lusty cowboys, gangsters, scantily clad women, or aliens. Howard Hughes' *The Outlaw* (1943) made Jane Russell's breasts a prominent selling point.

At the same time, even surefire gimmicks began to backfire. For *Mr. Blandings Builds His Dream House* (1948), RKO duplicated the plans for the house in question and raffled them off in one hundred cities. The house featured a state-of-the-art General Electric kitchen, and the lucky winners would get the entire house built for them, for free. There was just one problem: the house was designed by the RKO art department, not by real architects. There were no closets and no landings for the staircases. Plus, General Electric withdrew its support when it discovered that the director, H.C. Potter, had cut all the scenes featuring its kitchen and appliances. The whole episode came to an ugly conclusion when the winner of the "dream house" in Bel-Air, California, killed himself less than a year after his house was built because he couldn't afford to pay the taxes.

As the studios went into their death throes in the fifties, crumbling under an avalanche of bad management and losing theaters by the dozens, even the medium itself was exploited. A simple screen, a few comfortable seats, and a good story was no longer sufficient—people wanted convenience as well. Thus, the drive-in theater was born. The first drive-in theater in America opened in Camden, New Jersey, in 1933. Drive-ins were originally designed to sell automobile products, not movies. They were run by mechanics and parts distributors, as a friendly way to let your neighbors know where to get a good price on an oil pump. The real market for drive-ins didn't exist until after the Second World War, when families displaced to the suburbs discovered that driving into the theater was a lot easier than looking for a parking space downtown. And if you couldn't find or afford a babysitter, so what? Take the kids in their pajamas. "It makes no difference what you have on the screen," one New England drive-in operator exclaimed, "people come."

In 1946, there were 102 drive-in theaters in America; by 1958, there were more than four thousand. Concession stands offered complete dinners. There were playgrounds and miniature zoos for the kids and full-service laundromats for the parents. Asbury Park, New Jersey, featured a Fly-In theater, with spaces for twenty-five planes as well as five hundred cars. In Waltham, Massachusetts, patrons could row their way to a seat in a canoe-in theater.

What people saw on the screen changed in profound ways, as well. In 1952, *Bwana Devil* (United Artists) was the first 3-D feature. Two synchronized projectors passed the film through colored Polaroid filters, which, when the film was viewed through special paper glasses, provided the dubious thrill of objects seeming to be hurled at you from the screen. Crazed jungle monsters were followed by crazed aliens *(It Came from Outer Space,* Universal-International, 1953), demented murderers *(House of Wax,* Warner Bros., 1953), and, inevitably, Jane Russell *(The French Line,* RKO, 1953). A moderately successful attempt at a 3-D musical followed from—whom else but—MGM *(Kiss Me Kate,* 1953). Even Alfred Hitchcock gave it a try *(Dial M for Murder,* Warner Bros., 1954), but at this point the audiences had grown tired of wearing those uncomfortable glasses, and Hitchcock's mystery was shipped in the conventional, "flat" format. When 3-D eventually resurfaced, it did so primarily as camp *(Jaws 3D,* Universal, 1983).

The arrival of television sets in every home naturally inspired the technical geniuses who worked at the dying film studios to even greater heights of bombast. One inevitable result was CinemaScope, a wide-screen process that swamped the audience with size and sound. Making the screen bigger was not a new idea—people had been trying it out one way or another since the twenties—but without any real demand for change on the part of the public, there was no reason to persist. There was still no demand for change in the fifties, but by then, the industry had collapsed and rational business decisions were gone with the wind.

CinemaScope was merely the most successful version of several wide-screen processes that were all in competition with one another. A Frenchman named Henri Cretien designed and patented a system of special lenses and projectors that produced a screen image one-third wider than the traditional one. In 1953, Fox president Spyros Skouras stole Cretien's design, modified it slightly, named it CinemaScope, and unleashed it upon the world with *The Robe* (1953). Immediately there-

*E*xploitation rarely got any purer than this nearly fifty-foot-high Marilyn Monroe, for How to Marry a Millionaire *(Fox, 1953). For Fox's entry into the wide-screen wars, the studio chose bustiness over biblical recreations as its selling point.* Photograph courtesy of Photofest, New York.

after, copycat versions flooded the market. Cinerama used three cameras and three projectors, and left most audiences dizzy. Todd A-O (named for producer Mike Todd and his partner, the American Optical Company) lasted for two pictures. Howard Hughes' SuperScope ended up bouncing around with a few sub-B releases, and "Terrorscope," "Horrorscope," and "Naturama" lasted one picture each. In 1957, the development of Panavision, a reliable wide-screen lens that required no special screen or projector, killed off these quickie exploitation gimmicks for good.

Hollywood audiences have always been attracted by nonvisual gimmicks as well. For the film *Earthquake* (Universal, 1974), theaters added a low-level sound generator that produced slight tremors and called it "Sensurround." Short-lived gimmicks called "Aromarama" and "Smell-O-Vision" need no explanation. And then there was the Pope of Publicity—William Castle. Producer, director, master of publicity—William Castle's name is legendary among showmen past and present, the summation of all the old-fashioned gimmickry that came before him and the inspiration for all the media-driven, news-oriented public relations that was to come. In the words of director John Waters, a Castle acolyte, "William Castle was a publicity saint; a fame grifter who made public relations an art form and turned himself into his own biggest star. From the day he dropped out of high school to be Bela Lugosi's assistant (has there ever been a purer reason to quit school?) to his final days of insuring the life of the cockroach star of his newest film *Bug* for one million dollars, William Castle would do anything to get an audience."

William Castle was born William Schloss (German for "castle") in New York in 1914. He began his career as the assistant stage manager for Lugosi's theatrical tour of *Dracula* and once worked as an impressionist on a cruise ship. The publicity bug bit him in the early forties, when he convinced Orson Welles to sell him the lease on the Stony Creek Theater in Connecticut and then wrote the play for its premiere. When no one came, Castle broke in to his own theater, painted rude remarks on the walls, and complained loudly to the press. The crowds started coming. When the inevitable call came from Hollywood, Castle went. He bounced around Columbia and Universal for a while, directing B features, until the dissolution of the studio system opened the way for his career as an independent producer.

Castle's first production was *Macabre* (Castle/Allied Artists, 1958), a deliberate rip-off of the French masterpiece *Diabolique.* To sell the movie, Castle came up with the idea of insuring everybody in the world against death by fright. When Lloyd's of London tried to explain to him that the paperwork alone on such a policy would take several years, Castle settled for a policy that insured himself against claims. (The beneficiaries of anyone who died of fright during a screening of *Macabre* could sue William Castle and claim one thousand dollars.) "It would be terrible if someone actually did die," Castle announced, "but the publicity would be terrific." No one did, and it was, anyway.

Castle himself attended *Macabre's* opening in every city. In Minneapolis, he arrived at the theater inside a coffin in the back of a hearse. All went well until the moment came for Castle to pop out of the coffin and greet the audience. The lid of the coffin became stuck and Castle was trapped. Unfortunately, Castle's publicity manager, Johnny Flynn, and the few members of the audience who were paying attention concluded that the man's screams for help were part of the show. A frightened Castle killed the coffin routine for the next leg of the tour.

For *The Tingler* (Columbia, 1959), Castle installed tiny electric motors under randomly selected seats in any theater showing the film ("I'm going to buzz the asses of everyone in America," he proclaimed). Unfortunately, the cheap army surplus motors were so weak they barely hummed. The *New York Times* reported audience members sleeping through the buzzing, and one projectionist with a sense of humor turned the things on for an audience of elderly ladies deep in a matinee screening of *The Nun's Story.* Other Castle gimmicks included "Emergo," a skeleton on a string which burst out of a concealed box in *The House on Haunted Hill* (Castle/Allied Artists, 1958), and "Illusion-O," in which a special pair of glasses allowed you to see ghosts on the screen invisible to the naked eye. In *Homicidal* (Columbia, 1961), Castle's answer to *Psycho*, there was a scheduled "Fright Break"—sixty seconds of a clock ticking on the screen allowing anyone too scared to see the rest of the film to bolt and demand their money back. This backfired when enterprising kids figured out that if they sat through the picture twice, they could ask for their money back the second time and break even. For another picture, Castle put his newspaper ads among the obituaries.

To promote **The Good Earth** *(MGM, 1937), an enterprising operative created a rickshaw out of some old machine parts and the top half of a child's buggy, and hired a local farm boy and his sister to pull it through downtown St. Paul, Minnesota.* Photograph courtesy of Photofest, New York.

William Castle strangles himself on the set of *The Night Walker (Universal, 1964)*. Castle turned himself into his own best gimmick, giving bad publicity a good name.
Photograph courtesy of Photofest, New York.

Castle inspired legions of less talented (or, at least, less original) imitators. For *Witchcraft* (Robert Lippert/Jack Parsons, 1964), the producers distributed Day-Glo witch "deflectors." In *Rasputin, The Mad Monk* (Warners-Pathe, 1966), everyone got fake beards (blue for boys, pink for girls). Anyone who bought a ticket for *Dementia 13* (Roger Corman, 1963) was required to take a mental health test before each screening. The producers of *Beast of Blood* (Sceptre/Hemisphere, 1970) thoughtfully provided audience members with airsickness bags.

Meanwhile, Castle himself inched toward respectability of a sort. He managed to corral Joan Crawford for *Straight Jacket* (Columbia, 1963) and *I Saw What You Did* (Universal, 1965) after giving Miss Crawford full script, cast, and cameraman approval and arranging her personal tour. He even produced *Rosemary's Baby* for Paramount in 1968. But he still ended his career with that million-dollar cockroach.

Today, Hollywood promoters are content with the usual T-shirts, plastic toys, video games, and novelty items that glut the front end of supermarkets and the floor bins of discount drug chains. The closest things to the old movie fan magazines are *People* or *Entertainment Weekly,* which dabble in careless star-shots and candids that are sad approximations of anything resembling glamour. Even the trailers preceding today's feature films are as likely to be hooted as cheered. There's plenty of money being thrown into motion picture promotion, but not a heck of a lot of ingenuity.

Ingenuity was the keyword for the fabulous promotional gimmicks which rained down upon the grateful, happy moviegoer in the Golden Age of Hollywood. The men and women who dreamed up those toy guns, animal giveaway contests, and illegal lotteries, who arranged the personal appearances, wrote the radio copy, and dreamed up new ways to insinuate sex were nothing less than a national treasure. They should be cherished in our history books. We should raise their statues in our parks and in our city squares...

When you catch the spirit of selling, it's easy to get carried away. ★

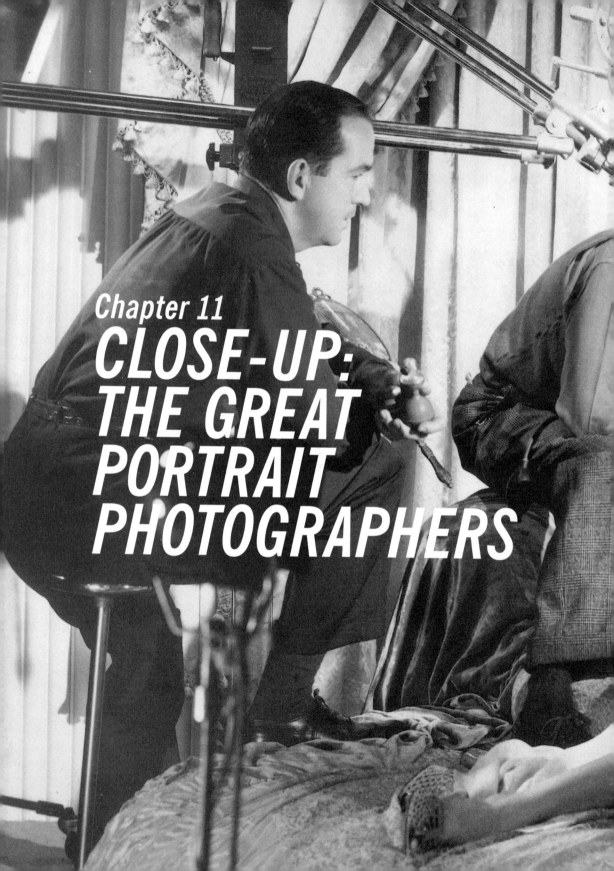

Chapter 11
CLOSE-UP: THE GREAT PORTRAIT PHOTOGRAPHERS

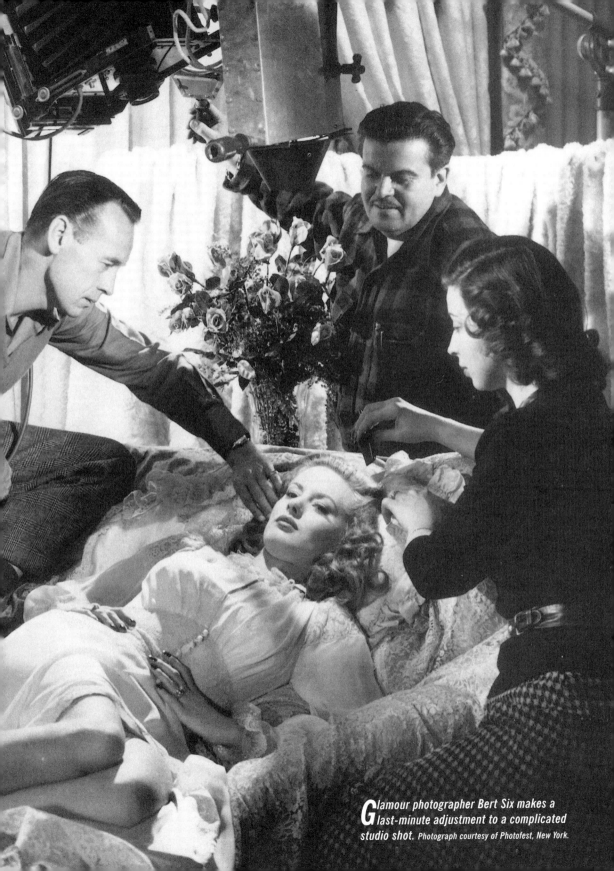

Glamour photographer Bert Six makes a last-minute adjustment to a complicated studio shot. *Photograph courtesy of Photofest, New York.*

With the portrait photograph, Hollywood came as close as it ever would to mimicking high art. The grand painted portrait, once reserved for kings and conquerors, could now be the province of mere actors, complete with *noblesse oblige* smile and the usual attributes of wealth and fame—furs, diamonds, and perfect teeth. Strangely enough, the same portrait also functioned as the cheapest and most popular vehicle for publicity ever invented. It is precisely this uneasy alliance of profundity and kitsch that makes the work of the great Hollywood portrait photographers so very alluring.

The earliest Hollywood star portraits, produced in the late teens and early twenties, were deliberate attempts to copy the prevailing, soft-focus style of art photography that was popular at the time. This style was named Secessionist, after a group of artists who exhibited their work at the annual international Secession art exhibit in Munich, beginning in 1903. Photographers such as Edward Steichen and Alfred Stieglitz saw the Secession in Europe and brought examples of it back to America just as the motion picture industry was expanding.

There were technical as well as aesthetic reasons for the rise of Hollywood portrait photography. Early sound cameras were far too noisy to allow for any sustained close-up work on the set. Close-ups of the stars, arranged to match the surrounding action, were routinely inserted into pictures, and the studios depended upon their portrait photographers to fill the screen with intensely lit, romantically hazy shots. Thus, what began as a practical solution to a technical problem turned into an entire cottage (or, in this case, bungalow) industry, as fans demanded portraits of their favorite stars. The "head shot," once entirely reserved for heads of state and men of science and letters, was now required of every actor, from the biggest star to the newest ingenue.

By the end of the twenties, all of the studios had established portrait galleries on their lots with talented photographers to run them. These men and women worked at the studio's beck and call, awaiting opportunities to catch a star, a supporting player, or a bit player as they ambled from the set to their dressing room. There were hundreds of photographers working in Hollywood at the time, producing thousands of portraits that were then duplicated by the millions and literally given away.

The publicity for every important picture included a portrait campaign. All the portrait work was scheduled before filming began, in order to allow the cast to concentrate on their acting and to leave the crew undisturbed on the set. The art department prepared the billboards and posters, and it was the portrait photographer's responsibility to pose the subjects in a manner that would produce a shot to match the existing artwork. At this point, the stars would be sent into the studio for straight portraits (makeup but no costumes), character portraits (full makeup and costumes, including character-based expressions), fashion shots (to be used in exploiting clothing and accessories), and advertising (including product endorsements).

As with everything else in Hollywood, portrait photography had a caste system, which developed over time in the same manner, and with the same results, as the star system. The lowest caste consisted of the "still men" (so-called even when they were women). Still men hung around the set, snapping candids or occasionally arranging quickly posed shots with a hand-held camera. These photographs would probably end up as decorations for the studio Christmas party or filler for the blank spots in a press book. Next up were the "in-house portraitists," who improvised studio work in abandoned corners of the lot when a good shot of a supporting cast member was needed. The top caste was reserved for very few people—the "contract artists" who owned their own (studio-supported) galleries off the lot and who arranged private, exclusive sittings with Hollywood's greatest stars.

Even among the best and most respected portrait photographers, there was no illusion that what they were doing was art, despite the glamorous milieu. Or, if it was "Art" with a capital "A" when it left the gallery, it was no longer considered such in the hands of the men in the front office. Studio executives judged the quality of the portrait photographers' work by weight, not by beauty. Millions of copies of a picture of the star dressed for his or her latest role needed to be mailed to the distributors, fan clubs, and newspapers before opening night. The photographs were reproduced as quickly and cheaply as possible. They were retouched by a battery of employees who cared not a whit about sensitivity and lighting, but only about whether Linda Darnell's nose looked too big. And they were copied and recopied until a reproduction bore little resemblance to the original negative, let alone the subject.

*A*nthony Ungrin photographing Shirley Temple. Ungrin was the classic example of the invaluable but unknown workhorse photographer that the studios employed. Ungrin had little choice as to who he would photograph, or when—he himself claimed he photographed Temple twenty times a day for over three years. *Photograph courtesy of Photofest, New York.*

The studio retouching experts were paid by the hour, so there was little incentive for them to leave well enough alone. They worked slowly and methodically. Pencils would remove wrinkles, teeth would be whitened and straightened (or even replaced), and starlets would regularly have their necks lengthened or their busts reduced or extended as needed. Each in-house photographer was expected to produce an average of nearly 300 negatives per day, and the lab would generate up to 1,500 prints. Little wonder that individuality was tossed to the wind.

Still, somehow, many of the greatest portrait photographers managed to create interesting—and often enduring—work. They tried to maintain control over the entire process from shooting to printing, so that the usual corners couldn't be cut. And they cultivated personal relationships with powerful stars that gave them some leeway when the studio lackeys started to tighten the screws. Many stars refused to be photographed by anyone except their personal favorites, who knew their faces virtually pore by pore. Though generally unknown to the world while they were working, these photographers now receive the kind of accolades once awarded only to the men and women they shot.

One of the most famous portrait photographers was George Hurrell, born in Kentucky in 1904. Hurrell studied to become a painter, but commissions were hard to come by, and he found steadier work helping Eugene Hutchinson, the most prominent society photographer in Chicago. Hurrell moved to Los Angeles in 1927, and friends there introduced him to Ramon Navarro, his first subject. Navarro loved Hurrell's work and introduced him to Norma Shearer, who was married to MGM producer Irving Thalberg. From that moment on, Hurrell's career at MGM was assured. His portraits of Shearer and Joan Crawford are rich and sensuous, the print texture crystalline. Hurrell was one of the few photographers allowed to work at Crawford's home, and their rapport and intimacy shines throughout his portraits of her.

Laszlo Willinger was also a popular MGM photographer and was dearly coveted by all of the studio's major stars. Willinger was an industrious Hungarian ex-patriot who often found the stars' and the studio's behavior amusing, if mystifying. "I remember once talking to Howard Strickling," he recalled to one interviewer, "and he said 'I want lots of glamour.' I said 'What's glamour?' And he said, 'You know, a sort of suffering look.' So there wasn't much laughing in these photos. You couldn't have happy sex. Sex and earnestness—together, these spelled glamour."

Willinger recounted the results of a publicity war between MGM's hottest stars during the time he was working on *The Women* (1939):

> Shearer would look at the prints first and say 'Gee, this is a beautiful picture of me, but I really don't like the way Joan Crawford looks.' And then Joan would have her turn, and we'd have the same thing. It's a wonder any pictures of them were released at all.
>
> One day, the principals took off from filming, just so we could shoot stills. The call was for ten a.m. I'm up there, ready—nobody. It's ten-thirty, eleven—still nobody. Finally Rosalind Russell turns up and says, 'Sorry, I'm late.' I told her, 'You're not late. You're the first one here.' I walked outside the stage that had been set up for the session.
>
> Finally, I saw Norma Shearer's car drive by. It slowed down. She looked out and continued driving around the block. A little behind her was Joan Crawford, who also slowed down, looked out, and drove on. I thought, 'What the hell is going on here?' I called Howard Strickling and told him, 'There are two stars outside driving around the stage and not coming in.' He said, 'Don't you know what they're doing? Shearer isn't going to come in before Crawford, and Crawford isn't going to come in before Shearer. The only thing I can do is stand in the middle of the street and stop them.' Which he did.

Clarence Sinclair Bull was Greta Garbo's favorite photographer throughout her short reign in Hollywood. Garbo never allowed herself to be photographed out of character, and she preferred one kind of lighting—very bright and angled on one side of her face. Very few stars got away with those kinds of demands, and very few photographers had the patience and understanding to allow it. It is almost entirely to Bull's credit that we have a photographic record of the face of one of Hollywood's most beautiful and enigmatic stars.

Although MGM dominated the portrait photography scene (as they

*C*larence Sinclair Bull was Garbo's favorite still man. Notice how Bull was clever enough to portray himself from below, giving his pipe and camera iconic significance and underlining his own stature as a sort of movie god. *Photograph courtesy of Photofest, New York.*

did every other aspect of the business in the Golden Age), photographers who worked at other studios could make a name for themselves by building a reputation for sensitive portrait work. Ernest Bachrach worked for RKO and became Katharine Hepburn's favorite photographer. Robert Coburn at Columbia drew accolades from Merle Oberon and Rita Hayworth. Ruth Harriet Louise, one of few women to succeed in this male-dominated field, had her own portrait gallery by the age of nineteen and specialized in "candid" and "action" studio work which gave her photos a distinctive, contemporary look. Art photographers such as Edward Steichen, Eugene Robert Richee, and Karl Struss all branched out into lucrative portrait work at one point or another in their careers. Anthony Ungrin made a career out of photographing the photogenic Shirley Temple.

John Engstead started in the publicity department at Paramount in 1926, working for Eugene Richee. He left Paramount in 1941 to become the house portraitist for *Harper's Bazaar.* Engstead developed many long and close relationships with the top stars in Hollywood. His memoirs, published in 1978, are filled with anecdotes recounting his life as a Hollywood portrait photographer.

While on assignment for *Harper's Bazaar,* Engstead recalled working with Joan Crawford at her home in Brentwood in 1943. The normally hyperfussy star suddenly appeared in the living room, her face flushed and without makeup. "Excuse my appearance," Crawford said. "I've been ironing. It's impossible to get help. So I do my own work." On another occasion, Crawford wanted Engstead to do a sitting of her in the middle of a heat wave and asked if the studio had air conditioning. It seems Miss Crawford needed the room kept at 65 degrees.

According to Engstead, Dietrich, too, was an expert at the art of exploitation. She would take hours to do her own makeup and never let anyone else touch it. She would spend another eight hours or longer with her dresser choosing her wardrobe. Engstead was present when the French couturier Jean Louis presented Dietrich with an invisible nylon body stocking for her 1953 Las Vegas engagement. "It was an achievement that ranked with the invention of the wheel and the cotton gin," he recalls. "When Marlene walked on the Las Vegas stage in that great Louis dress, it created a riot. There were dozens of press photographers in the room to record the incident and Marlene made sure, by exposing a great deal of her bosoms, that every single newspaper published her picture the next day. But her generosity in showing so much only lasted for the opening night. When I arrived a couple of days later to do a sitting for her, a few more beads had been added to her bodice."

In the end, Engstead offers a fascinating glimpse of how stars, working with knowledgeable portrait photographers, could create themselves, saying that "every personality in film always wanted to be as attractive an individual as possible. Each star strived to achieve distinction and each developed his or her own special 'look'...Gable found that wrinkling his forehead, squinting his eyes, and smiling produced a devastating look. Joan Crawford concentrated on intense eyes and a wide mouth. Gary Cooper used jaw muscles to show strength and found a little amusement in the face worked wonders."

Through the years, the stars' response to the ever-present and ever-demanding portrait photographers ran the gamut from wild enthusiasm to downright antipathy. The men, in general, didn't like posing under bright lights in heavy makeup. Spencer Tracy, James Cagney, Humphrey Bogart, and Clark Gable considered sitting for portraits "sissy stuff" and stayed as far away from the flash cameras as they could. Laszlo Willinger reported that Tracy would come into his studio, go under the lights, turn his head once to the left, then again to the right, and leave. Gary Cooper would fuss and fidget until Willinger was forced to settle for anything. The women, however, considered a portrait sitting the height of sophistication.

The epitome of the female star's compliance with the needs of the portrait photographer was also the most controversial—the pinup. Since photography was invented, people have been using pictures of sexy women (and sometimes men) to make money, and Hollywood, of course, was no exception. While star adoration and character development are eminently practical reasons for taking and distributing glamour photographs of stars, sex appeal was never far behind.

In the earliest years of the century, pinup girls were entirely adult entertainment. Sometimes nicknamed "calendar girls" because they often appeared as adornments to same, these earliest images of healthy womanhood were illustrations, not photographs, and thus the woman's fanciful and ideal qualities could be exaggerated without impropriety. Recall, however, that in the teens and early twenties, the movies them-

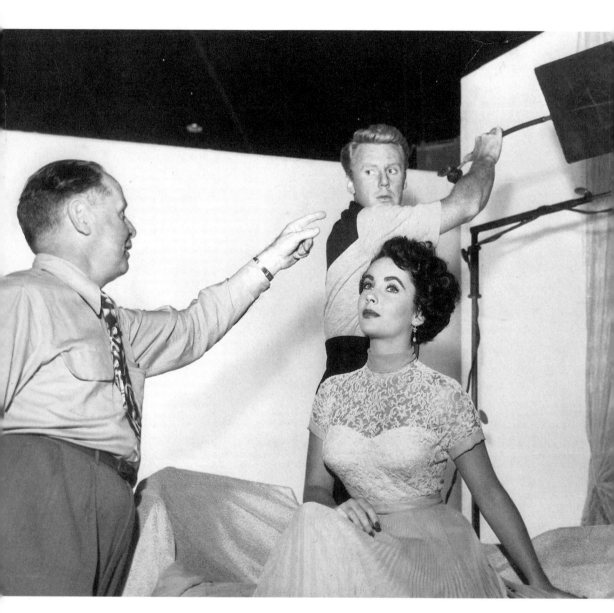

*T*he ever-enterprising Clarence Sinclair Bull gets Van Johnson to act as his assistant during this session with a gloriously beautiful Elizabeth Taylor. Photograph courtesy of Photofest, New York.

selves were considered less than respectable—both for the people working in front of the camera as well as those sitting in the theater. Idealism was practically required by law.

As both the cinema and sex drew greater public acceptance, they grew closer together. By the beginning of the World War II, Hollywood publicity and portrait photography became entwined in the form of the pinup. The kind of actress for whom it was unprofitable to pose for cheesecake, such as Greta Garbo or Katharine Hepburn, was fading in popularity, and those who were willing, such as Crawford, had grown older. What men wanted on the insides of their Army lockers, on the noses of their airplanes, and inside their wallets right next to their sweethearts were pictures of Betty Grable, Lana Turner, and Rita Hayworth. The old illusions that the great glamour photographs provided—bright lights, alluring sex, and exotic locales—were turning into reality. These popular pinup stars of the forties were actresses whose sex appeal was not at all muffled or subtle and whose talents were less thespian than photogenic. These publicity photographs—there was no longer any need to call them "art" or "glamour"—revealed a lot of flesh and a genial willingness to serve the needs of the nation just as much as any G.I.

By the end of the war, pinup and portrait photography had run its course as a useful tool of publicity. Popular picture magazines such as *Life* and *Look* promoted a new style of photography in which unposed shots were preferable to highly charged portraits, just as realistic subject matter was replacing fantasy on the screen. Furthermore, as the studios lost power, the stars gained it—and the stars were no longer willing to sit for long and carefully arranged portraits when they could just as usefully be photographed at a party or casually dining at home. Soon, the glamorous style that Hollywood had thought its own was being employed to sell everything from dog food to toasters. Being shiny and alluring was a condition more suited to a bedroom set than a working actress.

Stars still like to be photographed, and photographers still like to take pictures of stars—there's plenty of money and good publicity to be had in a two-page spread for *Entertainment Weekly* or a cover for *Vanity Fair*. But that perfect serenity—that silent, black-and-white moment when the star is frozen for all eternity—belongs to a different age, when illusions were shared and beauty was all. ★

The interior of Radio City Music Hall. The Hall featured a sixty-foot proscenium arch surrounded by acoustical tiles and 6,300 perfectly angled seats. Photograph courtesy of Photofest, New York.

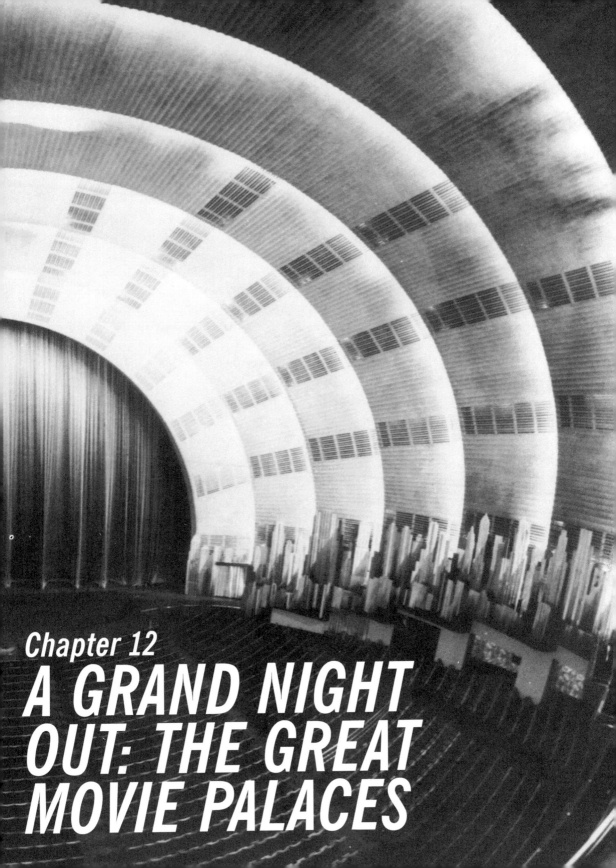

Chapter 12
A GRAND NIGHT OUT: THE GREAT MOVIE PALACES

In the first years of the twentieth century, the movies were just another side show. The earliest nickelodeons were hand-cranked viewing booths set up in the middle of arcades, right next to try-your-luck stands and carnival attractions. When the pictures moved out of the little black box and up onto the silver screen, businessmen quickly converted any space they could find. The first theaters were improvised in storefronts and alleyways.

Despite this makeshift milieu, movies were immediately and spectacularly popular. This immediately drew the attention of the fledgling tycoons. Louis B. Mayer originally owned a nickelodeon in Haverill, Massachusetts. Frustrated by films that were often unoriginal and poorly made, Mayer decided to investigate the costs of producing them himself. Similar dreams occurred to furriers like William Fox, bankers like Marcus Loew, and entrepreneurs like Jesse Lasky.

One great barrier to the expansion of the movie industry in the earliest years of the century was class. The majority of moviegoers were poverty-stricken immigrants. Pictures were considered poor people's entertainment, barely fit for "decent" folks and families. The young moguls making their first forays into the entertainment business quickly realized that if they were to attract a better class of patron, there needed to be a better class of theater. Thus, in a burst of greed-driven glee, the era of the great movie palace began.

From the end of the First World War to the beginning of the Depression, movie palaces were built in every city in America, on a scale never before seen and nearly unimaginable since. These monoliths of light were designed to entertain thousands of customers for over three hours every night. In the beginning, the movie palaces were modeled after the great European opera houses—classical and austere. But it was only a matter of time and money before theater designers moved into the realm of pure fantasy, making the movies the perfect place to go to forget your troubles and lose yourself in dreams.

Not all of this was done in the name of altruism, of course. For the millions of dollars the studios invested in their palaces, they were assured of earning scores of millions more in return. Each of the major players in Hollywood—MGM/Loew's, Paramount, and Fox—sewed up their own chains of theaters in all the major venues. These theaters were restricted to showing only their studio's product. Although the "smaller" big studios like Columbia and Warner Bros. survived by wheeling and dealing in the smaller markets, most of Hollywood's independent studios died. They had no place to show their pictures.

In New York, S.L. "Roxy" Rothapfel first built the Regent (1913) and then the Strand (1914) on Broadway. They were the first proscenium theaters built specifically for motion picture projection, with sight lines adjusted for the raised screen and padded seats for hours of comfort. Rothapfel's path to motion picture fortune and fame was typically tortuous. After serving a teenaged apprenticeship in the music halls lining New York's Union Square, Rothapfel joined the Marines. He was nearly thirty before he opened his first nickelodeon, in McKeesport, Pennsylvania. From there, he hooked up with the B.F. Keith vaudeville circuit, learning theater management from the biggest operation in the East. Within a year, he had built the Regent. Roxy possessed the fearlessness of a young man who had no idea what he was doing, and the Midas touch of being in the right place at the right moment.

At a time when the best of New York society would never dare venture above 34th Street, Rothapfel opened the Rialto in Times Square on April 21, 1916. The location was a colossal gamble—the bet was that the unfashionable address would be offset by the spectacular building. Roxy won the bet. The Rialto surpassed the Regent and the Strand in every way. The name of the theater was spelled out by over one thousand incandescent lights, rising above the marquee for nearly five stories and surmounted by a two-thousand-watt American eagle with a pair of Old Glories unfurling from his electric beak. Patrons passing through this portal on opening night were greeted by a staff of forty liveried ushers. There were two dozen live palms in the foyer and sixteen chandeliers hanging from the faux-Baroque ceiling. A fifty-piece orchestra entertained the crowd as it arrived. On the bill: a scenographic short about Venice, Douglas Fairbanks in *The Good Bad Man,* a musical interlude from noted baritone Alfred De Manby, a Fatty Arbuckle comedy, and, finally, a two-reeler based on Richard Strauss's symphonic poem *Till Eulenspiegel.*

The Rialto, magnificent as it was, was almost immediately surpassed by the Rivoli, which opened on December 28, 1917, two blocks

Roxy Theatre, New Yor

The Roxy Theatre, New York. The Roxy was one of the last great urban movies palaces built in America—a hodgepodge of Oriental, Arabic, and Western architectural styles whose emphasis was on scale (big) and glamour (exotic). Photograph courtesy of the Museum of the City of New York, New York.

to the north, on Broadway at 45th Street. The Rivoli, not lacking in modesty, was modeled on the Parthenon in Athens. This, in turn, was followed by the Capitol, at 51st Street, which, with a capacity of 5,300, was the largest theater in the world at the time. Such was the cachet of the premiere of a new Broadway picture house that George Gershwin and Irving Caesar wrote an entire suite of songs for the occasion, including "Come to the Moon" and a little throwaway they called "Swanee."

Most of these houses were designed by the architect Thomas Lamb. Lamb's classical style was well-suited to the earliest age of the movie palace, where the emphasis was on elegance and spaciousness. As well as the Rialto and the Capitol, Lamb designed San Francisco's Fox, generally considered the classic early picture palace. Later, when relative austerity gave way to complete abandon, and "gaudier" and "cheaper" were the words of the day, Lamb designed two extraordinary "wedding-cake" theaters—Loew's 72nd Street and Loew's 175th Street, both in upper Manhattan.

Meanwhile, on the West Coast, movie palace design was taking a gigantic leap forward under the inspiration of Sid Grauman. Starting with one theater on Market Street in San Francisco in 1905, Grauman slowly began working his way down the coast, building increasingly larger and more ornate houses along the way. California's architecture was much less influenced by European styles than New York's, and the men who designed Grauman's palaces felt no need to connect their buildings with either architectural history or the surrounding landscape.

The result of this iconoclasm was Grauman's Egyptian Theatre, which opened on October 18, 1922, and Grauman's Chinese Theatre, which opened on May 18, 1927. As their names suggest, these theaters were grandiose parodies of ancient building styles, designed to enhance the unreality of the Hollywood universe. For his theaters, Grauman created the first "premiere," hiring limousines for the stars, crisscrossing the sky with incandescent beams of light, laying down a red carpet, and renting gardens of exotic flowers. The Chinese Theatre was barely finished for opening night. While a team of workers was still laying fresh concrete along the sidewalk in front of the box office, Norma Talmadge thought it might be amusing to leave her handprints in the wet clay, and one of Hollywood's great publicity gimmicks and tourist attractions was born. Now Cinamerica/Mann, which owns the Chinese, is planning to build full-scale replicas of the famous kitsch palace all across America. Meanwhile, the Egyptian, thanks to a $13 million renovation, is now the home of the American Cinematheque, a catch-all organization for film restoration, education, and development.

The most memorable excesses of the Golden Age of the movie palace were saved as a flourish for its end. The last two major palaces built in America were the most famous: the Roxy Theatre and Radio City Music Hall.

The Roxy was designed by Walter W. Ahlschlager and decorated by Harold W. Rambisch. By the time it opened, on March 11, 1927, it had cost over $10 million to build, the costliest theater ever. With a capacity of 6,200, it dwarfed the Capitol, one block to the east. Everything about the Roxy was designed to impress. The lobby columns were copied from Saint Peter's in Rome, the box seats from Santa Maria Novella in Florence, and the archways in the orchestra from Mont Saint Michel in France. The lobby was laid with the largest oval rug in the world—weighing in at over two and a half tons, it needed a tractor to lift it for cleaning. There were five floors of dressing rooms, a stable for animals (used mostly during the annual Christmas pageant) a private hospital, sixty bathrooms, and a broadcast studio on the top of the building large enough to hold a hundred-piece orchestra.

In Ben M. Hall's beautifully written history of the Golden Age of the movie palace, *The Best Remaining Seats* (published in 1961, just before most of the theaters he wrote about were demolished), the author describes the delicious scene at the Roxy's opening night, as flappers, businessmen, bums, and housewives jostled each other on the street for a view of the arrival of the hoi polloi. Hall reports that the procession of touring cars and Checker Cabs so completely blocked Sixth Avenue that the passengers eventually climbed out in the middle of the street and fought their way through the traffic to the brand-new theater marquee, crushing the police barricades which were set up to contain the crowds but were merely escalating the commotion.

Hall humorously recalls how a certain Mr. and Mrs. H.W. Llewellyn, of Newark, New Jersey, got to the Roxy early. "The Llewellyns had the foresight in November 1925 to send a blank check requesting two seats for opening night," he writes. "Now, a year and a half later and bearing engraved cards instead of tickets, they stood at the bronze doors of the Cathedral of the Motion Picture, blinking in the glare of the floodlights. Then, as a barrage of photographers' flash powder went off and the crowd began to shout, the Llewellyns were swept inside on a wave of spangles, spit curls, and opera hats. For a while they bobbed around in the Rotunda, a little floating island of delighted disbelief, until finally they were swallowed up in the dim vastness of the auditorium, to be seen no more."

In its day, the Roxy was one of the most spectacular public buildings in the world. Sadly, it is gone—destroyed in 1960 to make way for a parking lot (and now, a hotel). But it still stands in the memory of anyone who lived in New York City and was born between the turn of the century and the end of the Korean War. Songs have been written about it ("Bring Back the Roxy," by Michael Brown, sung in Julius Monk's 1962 revue *Dressed to the Nines)*. Musical comedies have been created in homage to it (Stephen Sondheim's *Follies,* about a reunion of showgirls on an old, dilapidated stage). Even the author of this book, too young to have visited the Roxy while it stood, still vividly recalls being brought to the ruins at the age of five and being told by his father: "Remember!"

The Roxy was destined to be challenged and surpassed—but only once, and, of course, by Roxy Rothapfel himself. On December 27, 1932, Radio City Music Hall opened on the corner of Sixth Avenue and 50th Street, at the edge of the brand-new Rockefeller Center. There were twenty-five acts on the opening night bill, including the legendary vaudeville team of Weber and Fields (who came out of retirement for the occasion), Fields' daughter Dorothy and her songwriting partner Jimmy McHugh, and the Flying Wallendas. The management received over 100,000 requests for tickets, and the last act on the bill didn't come off the stage until three in the morning. The next day, even the usually cranky Ed Sullivan was moved to write in his column that Radio City was "as significant in our generation as the pyramids."

Radio City was perfectly positioned to exploit its role as the premier launching pad for the worldwide success of a big new film. It was the centerpiece of a conglomerate of entertainment businesses. RCA owned the building and also built the radio sets that everybody needed to listen to Walter Winchell hype Radio City's shows. RCA also owned RKO, so that RKO pictures could compete with the big boys in a big-name venue. With a screen seventy-five feet wide and thirty-five feet high, every picture projected at Radio City looked magnificent.

Furthermore, unlike most of the other movie palaces built in America, Radio City was modern. No muted candelabras, Greek columns, traditional murals, or marble fauns here. The designer, Donald Deskey, firmly believed in using modern materials in the contemporary Art Deco style. All the paintings, all the furniture, even the choice of fabric for the seats was personally selected and coordinated by Deskey. He commissioned great artists to create new works exclusively for Radio City. Stuart Davis painted a modern mural (logically, if bizarrely, entitled "Men Without Women") for one of the men's smoking lounges. Ezra Winter's murals for the grand staircase and Edward Caldwell's two-ton chandeliers were dazzling and raucous. Another smoking lounge included a mural on the history of tobacco rendered entirely in aluminum foil and donated by the R.J. Reynolds Company.

Then there were the Rockettes. It may be hard to believe, but the Rockettes existed before Radio City. They were created and directed by Russell Markert, who first thought of the idea of step-coordinated dancing girls while he was working on the Publix vaudeville circuit in the 1920s. Known as the Roxyettes, the girls made their first New York appearance at the Roxy in 1927. Roxy pulled them from his self-named theater and added them (still called the Roxyettes) to the opening day bill at Radio City, where they have remained ever since.

The Rockettes tradition has never been broken. The original team of sixteen girls stayed together for ten years, and until the seventies the entire corps never expanded beyond thirty-two—sixteen onstage, sixteen in the wings. Altogether, there have been approximately four hundred Rockettes. Markert himself choreographed the Rockettes' routines for nearly forty years. Since then, almost every director has been a retired member of the corps. Over the years, the Rockettes have been coaxed into every costume imaginable—from astronauts and dolls to furniture, and horses.

In their heyday, the movie palaces offered democratic luxury and entertainment at its most professional, all for a very modest cost. Besides the comfortable seats, air-conditioning, and enormous screens,

One lone man surveys the glorious splendor of the lobby at Radio City Music Hall. Somehow, Radio City stumbled through the assault of television, the long years of bad movies and terrible stage shows, eviction threats, hovering wrecking balls, and nearly complete public indifference to survive as the last remaining old-style movie palace. Although the elegance has faded a bit and Holiday Extravaganzas have replaced everyday film fare on the bill, the room is still impressive and the Rockettes still swing their legs nightly. Photograph courtesy of the Museum of the City of New York, New York, Wurts Brothers Collection.

Salvatore Santaella and his orchestra play for the premiere of Lost Horizon (Columbia, 1937) at the Hollywood 4 Star Theater, March 1937. In the Golden Age of Hollywood, premieres were the parties of choice for the stars, for the audience, and for the performers. Before television brought entertainment into everyone's living room, a night at the movies would be one of the only ways to hear your favorite band, laugh along with your favorite comedian, or have a true night on the town.

Photograph courtesy of Photofest, New York.

most palaces featured live music (either an orchestra or at least an organist). Rudy Vallee began his career singing in front of the curtain at the Brooklyn Paramount. Myrna Loy and Janet Gaynor were "Sunkist Beauties," shilling for orange juice on the Marco & Fanchon vaudeville theater circuit. Max Baer demonstrated shadowboxing from the stage of the Capitol; Ginger Rogers was a chorus girl at the Paramount. Every big theater in America booked entertainment for opening night and beyond. Shows would begin at 11:00 A.M. and continue until nearly midnight.

Concessions, too, were a big part of any palace's marketing ploys. At first, it was considered impolite to eat in a theater—after all, they don't do that in the legitimate houses, do they? But the theater managers quickly noticed their patrons running out in the middle of screenings to get a soda pop or a candy bar from the five-and-ten across the street. They tried candy barkers in the aisles between screenings, as if it was a ballpark, but that merely caused traffic jams. Eventually the current system of lobby stands was accepted. The first Coke was served at the Roxy in 1947, and by the fifties, drive-ins offered complete dinners.

The large theaters were also an important part of every big city's economic health. Hundreds of people would be employed in one theater alone, selling tickets or concessions, playing in the band, cleaning up, or ushering. Every boy wanted to be an usher—to be issued a uniform and see every film (Roxy's ushers had classrooms, summer camps, and in-house tutors). As perhaps the only affordable source of entertainment in town, movie palaces provided a safe and comfortable place for kids to go after school, and for families to attend together on weekends.

Throughout the twenties and thirties, movie palaces were one of America's premier democratic institutions. Architect George Rapp, who with his brother designed the Brooklyn Paramount as well as the Oriental and the Palace in Chicago, summed up most patrons' feelings when he wrote about the moviegoing experience of his day:

> Watch the eyes of a child as it enters the portals of our great theatres and treads the pathway into fairyland. Watch the bright light in the eyes of the tired shopgirl who hurries noiselessly over carpets and sighs with satisfaction as she walks amid furnishings which once delighted the hearts of queens. See the toil-

worn father whose dreams have never come true, and look inside his heart as he finds strength and rest within the theatre. There you have the answer to why picture theatres are so palatial.

Here is a shrine to democracy where there are no privileged patrons. The wealthy rub elbows with the poor—and are better for this contact. Do not wonder, then, at the touches of Italian Renaissance, executed in glazed polychrome terra cotta, or at the lobbies and foyers adorned with replicas of precious master-pieces of another world, or at the imported marble wainscoting or the richly ornamented ceilings with motifs copied from mas-terpieces of Germany, France, or Italy, or at the carved niches, the cloistered arcades, the depthless mirrors, and the great sweeping staircases. These are not impractical attempts at showing off. These are part of a celestial city—a cavern of many-colored jewels, where iridescent lights and luxurious fittings heighten the expectation of pleasure. It is richness unabashed, but richness with a reason.

The end came with the Depression. As people migrated out of town looking for work, the movie palaces suddenly began playing to empty houses. Gimmicks such as double features and giveaways pumped things up for a little while, but when the vaudeville circuits dried up and the live acts disappeared from the bill, there was even less reason to go to the movies. The situation improved a bit during World War II, but came to a swift and final conclusion immediately thereafter. The gov-ernment finally won its antitrust suit against the studios (they had been fighting for years), forcing the studios to sell their theaters. The popula-tion of the nation was shifting rapidly from the decaying urban centers, where all the palaces were located, to suburbia, where new theaters with ample parking and lower overhead costs could be built quickly and cheaply. People started staying home and watching television.

Today, there are fewer moviegoers alive who recall the old picture palaces. A new generation, raised on videotape and the tiny box theaters of the multiplex, are being enticed back to the movies by promises of arena-type seating, quadrophonic Dolby sound systems, and take-out restaurants right in the lobby. A few of the larger chains, such as the

In a world barely recovered from the Depression and currently shattered by war, it was reassuring to watch the stars arrive at a movie premiere—even if the movie itself was a harsh reminder of reality, David O. Selznick's tearjerker Since You Went Away *(United Artists, 1944)* Photograph courtesy of Photofest, New York.

An elderly usher stands guard at the entrance to the Los Angeles Theatre, circa 1943. Within a very few years, scenes like this would not have needed to be staged—the empty balconies and abandoned marquees would be all too real. Photograph courtesy of Photofest, New York.

venerable Loew's, are attempting to create "mini-palaces" that reside within multiplexes but have old-fashioned, "exotic" marquees.

Today, it is very hard to know what those first generations must have felt when they walked into a movie palace. We can try to imagine that first blast of ice-cold air, the smell of the popcorn, and the dull roar of the music coming from high up a marble staircase. We think we know how a silver screen as wide as the side of a building must have looked to a kid who had until then never seen a picture bigger than a comic book. We imagine hundreds and even thousands of people in the room with us, sharing our experience and reinforcing our sense of the world. All this— once novel, once inspiring, once ennobling—is gone.

Ben Hall ends *The Best Remaining Seats* with a eulogy, as relevant today as when it was written, nearly forty years ago. He writes, "For the dwindling number of genuine movie palaces that still open their doors, the going is getting tough. A few have had their faces lifted by uninspired interior decorators whose idea of cosmetic surgery is to smother every vestige of ornament, from proscenium to projection booth, in bolts of neutral-colored fiberglass." Hall laments the once graceful French curve of the New York Paramount's marquee, replaced by a frosted-glass trapezoid with plastic letters (the building was subsequently reincarnated as a luxury hotel). He points out that an escalator was built right up the middle of the Capitol's famous white marble stairs (now the Capitol, too, is gone). "Out in Hollywood," he concludes, "the foliated-gold interior of the Pantages Theatre resembles a yard-goods department and its seating has been drastically reduced to make the delegations who come to see the latest version of the Bible according to CinemaScope feel less lonely." Finally, Hall's tone turns serious and apocalyptic: "The clouds that once floated over a thousand balconies have drifted away for good," he cries. "The machines broke years ago. One by one the stars have blinked out, their tiny bulbs blackened . . . dead stars in the cold outer space of grimy atmospheric ceilings. Supermarkets, garages, and apartment houses now loom where the once-proud Granadas, Strands, Rivolis, Tivolis, and Orientals stood."

In a photo on the next page, Gloria Swanson stands in the ruins of the Roxy, her hands outstretched in supplication to an unseeing God. ★

*O*ld Hollywood's last splash: Eddie Fisher shows off for an obliging photographer moments before splashing into the Desert Inn swimming pool, circa 1950. *Photograph courtesy of Photofest, New York.*

AFTERWORD

*T*roy Donahue and Connie Stevens hit the road in support of Susan Slade (Warner Bros., 1961). By the beginning of the sixties, the studios were emitting their last gasp of old-style publicity. Very soon, the bigger stars in better movies would (and could) demand much more than airfare—including the right to stay home. Personal appearances and publicity tours were things of the past.
Photograph courtesy of Photofest, New York.

*T*he death of Old Hollywood was inevitable, but it came very slowly. No one wanted it to die—not the millionaires who made or produced or starred in the pictures, not the fans who filled the balconies, and certainly not the people whose small livelihoods depended upon the movies: the theater employees, the owners and workers in the downtown shops and stores that surrounded the theaters, and the people who worked in related industries such as cosmetics, publishing, fashion, music, and finance.

The first signs of impending doom began to appear as early as 1921. The Federal Trade Commission filed suit to prevent the studios from owning chains of exclusive theaters, a suit which took eleven years to settle and wasn't enforced until the Supreme Court intervened in 1948. The Production Code attempted to keep pictures from reflecting too much reality. There was at first a consensus to at least appear to abide by its rules, until a generation of moviegoers, experiencing real racial and moral problems during the Second World War, no longer believed that ignorance was bliss. Unions, which had done so much to better the lives of millions of Americans during the worst years of labor exploitation in the nineteenth and early twentieth centuries, now found themselves considered subversive. Top writers and directors were labeled as Communists and blacklisted.

When television antennae began sprouting on the roofs of homes across America, Old Hollywood ceased to exist. At first, the studios tried to ignore the upstart entertainer, hoping it would go away. When benign neglect failed to cut into TV sales, and box office receipts continued to decline, theater managers put television sets in their lobbies and hoped for bad reception. No luck. Finally the studios decided it was time to sleep with the enemy. In April 1953, Fox released its entire catalog to television. MGM was quick to follow. All of Warner Bros.' pictures went to ABC in March 1955. "The Late Show" and "The Late, Late Show" were born. Once Americans had adjusted to watching movies on television, it was harder than ever to get them to come out to the theaters, despite 3-D, Cinerama, and Jane Russell. The first duplex opened in Kansas City in 1963; the first quadraplex in 1966. Sextuplets followed in 1969, a dozen by the early eighties. Then videotape. Finis glamour.

Now some multiplexes in the biggest cities are reopening with faux movie-palace designs and gourmet snack counters, trying to recreate the old movie palace ambience for what used to be the price of an entire week's groceries. Stars occasionally misbehave or intermarry to advance their careers—low-budget and usually short-lived attempts to create some Hollywood glitz around a failed movie project. Every couple of years, a film comes along which ignites the public interest in the old way, like *Star Wars* (Fox/Lucasfilms, 1977) or *Titanic* (Fox/Paramount, 1997). But they are few and far between.

In the end, Hollywood—the Hollywood of the Golden Age, in black-and-white or Technicolor, with more stars than there are in heaven—was destroyed by its own success. The industry wanted the world to resemble a Hollywood movie and so, inevitably, did everybody else. But this never was true, and soon enough, the world figured that out, too. Gradually the fantasy world of Hollywood learned to accommodate a little more of the real world. Now they co-exist, but neither one resembles what it used to be.

The ultimate embodiment of this topsy-turvy world was Ronald Reagan. While Reagan was merely an actor, he epitomized the best of the Old Hollywood can-do, just-folks, anyone-can-be-a-star mentality. Then he exploited his Hollywood persona and succeeded in getting elected governor of California and then leader of the free world. Now Hollywood was running America while the motion picture industry was talking about nuclear war, social injustice, and sexual liberation. This was a long way from Franklin Delano Roosevelt and Shirley Temple.

Or was it?

Never underestimate the power of images—they can create very attractive illusions. Perhaps the era of innocent exploitation is gone forever, but people still want to be scared out of their wits, to see a good woman or man triumph, or to watch two people fall in love. These stories aren't sold to us with quite the same shameless exuberance or with such original finesse anymore, but we still buy them, just the same. ★

*J*ulie Andrews poses for George Hurrell on the set of Star! (Fox, 1968). Tastes were changing and the era of the Hollywood musical was nearly over when Andrews made this film biography of the English stage performer Gertrude Lawrence. Photograph courtesy of Photofest, New York.

*B*elles of the ball: Ava Gardner, Irene Dunne, Diana Lynn, and Loretta Young patiently pose for a *B*portrait. Photograph courtesy of Photofest, New York.

BIBLIOGRAPHY

PRIMARY SOURCES

Castle, William. *Step Right Up!: I'm Gonna Scare the Pants Off America.* New York: Pharos Books, 1992.

Cinema press books from the original studio collections. Originals held in the collection of the Wisconsin Center for Film and Theater Research. Microfilms published by Research Publications, Reading, England, 1988.

Dietz, Howard, and Howard Strickling. *Who's Who at Metro-Goldwyn-Mayer.* Culver City, California: Metro-Goldwyn-Mayer, 1940.

Engstead, John. *Star Shots: Fifty Years of Pictures and Stories by One of Hollywood's Greatest Photographers.* New York: Dutton, 1978.

Goodman, Ezra. *The Fifty-Year Decline and Fall of Hollywood.* New York: Simon and Schuster, 1961.

Green, Abel and Joe Laurie, Jr. *Show Biz from Vaude to Video.* New York: Henry Holt, 1951.

Hendricks, Bill, and Howard Waugh. *Charles "Chick" Lewis Presents the Encyclopedia of Exploitations.* New York: Showmen's Trade Review, 1937.

Hopper, Hedda, and James Brough. *The Whole Truth and Nothing But.* Garden City, New York: Doubleday, 1963.

LeRoy, Mervyn, and Alyce Canfield. *It Takes More Than Talent,* with an introduction by Louis B. Mayer. New York: Knopf, 1953.

Lewis, Judy. *Uncommon Knowledge.* New York: Pocket Books, 1994.

MacNamara, Paul. *Those Were the Days, My Friend: My Life in Hollywood with David O. Selznick and Others.* Metuchen, New Jersey: Scarecrow Press, 1993.

MGM Data Book, compiled by George C. Maurer. New York: Loew's, Inc. 1956.

Nelson, Chris. *Interview with Max Youngstein.* Conducted in 1989, unpublished.

Parsons, Louella. *Tell It to Louella.* New York: Putnam, 1961.

_____. *The Gay Illiterate.* Garden City, New York: Doubleday, Doran and Co., 1944.

Powdermaker, Hortense. *Hollywood, the Dream Factory: An Anthropologist Looks at the Movie-Makers.* Boston: Little, Brown, 1950.

Ricketson, Frank H., Jr. *The Management of Motion Picture Theatres.* New York: McGraw-Hill, 1938.

St. Johns, Adela Rogers. *Love, Laughter, and Tears: My Hollywood Story.* Garden City, New York: Doubleday, 1978.

Thorp, Margaret Farrand. *America at the Movies.* New Haven: Yale University Press, 1939.

OTHER SOURCES

Balio, Tino, ed. *The American Film Industry.* Madison, Wisconsin: University of Wisconsin Press, 1985.

Balio, Tino. *Grand Design: Hollywood As a Modern Business.* New York: Macmillan, 1990.

Beauchamp, Cari and Henri Behar. *Hollywood on the Riviera: The Inside Story of the Cannes Film Festival.* New York: William Morrow and Co., 1992.

Bridges, Herb. *"Frankly, My Dear"—Gone with the Wind Memorabilia.* Macon, Georgia: Mercer University Press, 1986.

Celebration and Remembrance: Commemorative Textiles in America. North Andover, Massachusetts: Museum of American Textile History, 1990.

Edwards, Anne. *Shirley Temple: American Princess.* London: Collins, 1988.

Friedrich, Otto. *City of Nets: A Portrait of Hollywood in the 1940's.* New York: Harper & Row, 1986.

Goodwin, Betty. *Hollywood du Jour: Lost Recipes of Legendary Hollywood Haunts.* Santa Monica: Angel City Press, 1993.

Hall, Ben M. *The Best Remaining Seats: The Story of the Golden Age of the Movie Palace.* New York: Clarkson Potter, 1961.

Kreuger, Miles, ed. *The Movie Musical from Vitaphone to 42nd Street, As Reported in a Great Fan Magazine.* New York: Dover Publications, 1975.

McGee, Mark Thomas. *Beyond Ballyhoo: Motion Picture Promotion and Gimmicks.* Jefferson, North Carolina: McFarland, 1989.

Stones, Barbara. *America Goes to the Movies: 100 years of Motion Picture Audiences.* North Hollywood, California: The National Association of Theatre Owners, 1993.

Wilkerson, Tichi and Marcia Borie. *The Hollywood Reporter: The Golden Years.* New York: Coward-McCann, 1984.

Index

Movie Story *was one of the many Hollywood fan magazines that proliferated in the thirties and forties. It featured "novelizations" of current releases as bait to lure customers into the theaters.* Photograph courtesy of Photofest, New York.